First World War
and Army of Occupation
War Diary
France, Belgium and Germany

3 CAVALRY DIVISION
Headquarters, Branches and Services
General Staff Appendices to 1141
3 April 1917 - 30 June 1917

WO95/1142/3

The Naval & Military Press Ltd
www.nmarchive.com
Published in association with The National Archives

Published by

The Naval & Military Press Ltd

Unit 10 Ridgewood Industrial Park,

Uckfield, East Sussex,

TN22 5QE England

Tel: +44 (0) 1825 749494

www.naval-military-press.com

www.nmarchive.com

This diary has been reprinted in facsimile from the original. Any imperfections are inevitably reproduced and the quality may fall short of modern type and cartographic standards.

© Crown Copyright
Images reproduced by permission of The National Archives, London, England, 2015.

Contents

Document type	Place/Title	Date From	Date To
Miscellaneous			
Miscellaneous	6th. Cav. Bde. Appx. 1	03/04/1917	03/04/1917
Miscellaneous	March Table-3rd. Cavalry Division.		
Miscellaneous	6th. Cav. Bde. App 2	05/04/1917	05/04/1917
Miscellaneous	March Table-3rd Cavalry Division. April 7th.		
Miscellaneous	March Table-3rd Cavalry Division. 8th. April		
Miscellaneous	6th Cav Bde. App 3	07/04/1917	07/04/1917
Operation(al) Order(s)	3rd Cavalry Division Concentration Order No. 1 App 4	08/04/1917	08/04/1917
Operation(al) Order(s)	3rd. Cavalry Division Concentration Order No. 2 Appendix 5	08/04/1917	08/04/1917
Miscellaneous	Medical Arrangements For Z Day.	08/04/1917	08/04/1917
Miscellaneous	6th. Cavalry Brigade. App 6	08/04/1917	08/04/1917
Operation(al) Order(s)	3rd Cavalry Division Operation Order No. 1 Appx 7	08/04/1917	08/04/1917
Miscellaneous	3rd Cavalry Division Provisional Defence Scheme. Appendix 10	17/05/1917	17/05/1917
Miscellaneous	3rd Cavalry Division Defence Scheme. Appendix 11	21/05/1917	21/05/1917
Miscellaneous	6th. Cavalry Brigade. Appendix A.	23/05/1917	23/05/1917
Miscellaneous	Orders For Relief. Appendix 12	22/05/1917	22/05/1917
Miscellaneous	6th. Cav. Bde. Appendix 12	22/05/1917	22/05/1917
Miscellaneous	3rd. Cavalry Division Summary Of Intelligence 11 a.m. 24th- to 11 a.m. 25th. May 1917 Appendix 24	25/05/1917	25/05/1917
Miscellaneous	3rd. Cavalry Division Intelligence Summary from 11 a.m. 25/5/17 to 11 a.m. 26/5/1917	26/05/1917	26/05/1917
Miscellaneous	3rd. Cavalry Division Intelligence Summary from 11 a.m. 26/5/17 to 11 a.m. 27/5/1917	27/05/1917	27/05/1917
Miscellaneous	3rd. Cavalry Division Intelligence Summary from 8 a.m. 27th. to 8 a.m. 28th. May, 1917	28/05/1917	28/05/1917
Miscellaneous	3rd. Cavalry Division Intelligence Summary from 8 a.m. 28th. to 8 a.m. 29th. May, 1917	29/05/1917	29/05/1917
Miscellaneous	3rd. Cavalry Division Intelligence Summary for 24 hours-8 a.m. 29th. 8 a.m. 30th. May, 1917	30/05/1917	30/05/1917
Miscellaneous	3rd Cavalry Division Summary of Intelligence For 24hours- 8 a.m. 30th to 8 a.m. 31st May, 1917	31/05/1917	31/05/1917
Miscellaneous	3rd Cavalry Division Fortnightly Summary, Period Ending 31st May, 1917	31/05/1917	31/05/1917
Miscellaneous	3rd Cavalry Division Intelligence Summary for 24 hours from 8 a.m. 31st. May, to 8 a.m. 1st. June 1917	01/06/1917	01/06/1917
Miscellaneous	Annexe to 3rd. Cavalry Division Summary 1st. June, 1917		
Miscellaneous			
Miscellaneous	3rd. Cavalry Division Intelligence Summary for 24 hours- from 8 a.m. 1st. June to 8 a.m. 2nd. June, 1917. Appendix 10	02/06/1917	02/06/1917
Miscellaneous	3rd. Cavalry Division Intelligence Summary for 24 hours-8 a.m. 2nd. to 8 a.m. 3rd. June, 1917.	03/06/1917	03/06/1917
Miscellaneous	Annexe to 3rd. Cavalry Division Summary 3rd. June, 1917		
Miscellaneous	3rd Cavalry Division Intelligence Summary Period 8 a.m. 3rd to 8 a.m. 4th June, 1917	04/06/1917	04/06/1917

Miscellaneous	3rd Cavalry Division Intelligence Summary for 24 hours- from 8 a.m. 4th. to 8 a.m. 5th June, 1917	05/06/1917	05/06/1917
Miscellaneous	3rd Cavalry Division Intelligence Summary, 8 a.m. 5th to a.m. 6th June, 1917	06/06/1917	06/06/1917
Miscellaneous	3rd. Cavalry Division Intelligence Summary for 24 hours from 8 a.m. 6th. to 8 a.m. 7th. June, 1917	07/06/1917	07/06/1917
Miscellaneous	Addendum to 3rd. Cavalry Division Summary for 24 hours from 8. a.m. 6th to 8 a.m. 7th. June 1917	07/06/1917	07/06/1917
Miscellaneous	3rd Cavalry Division Intelligence Summary for 24 hours from 8 a.m. 7th. to 8 a.m. 8th June, 1917		
Miscellaneous	3rd Cavalry Division Intelligence Summary for 24 hours 8 a.m. 8th. to 8 a.m. 9th June, 1917	09/06/1917	09/06/1917
Miscellaneous		08/06/1917	08/06/1917
Miscellaneous	3rd Cavalry Division Intelligence Summary for 24 hours- from 8 a.m. 9th to 8 a.m. 10th June, 1917	10/06/1917	10/06/1917
Miscellaneous	3rd Cavalry Division Intelligence Summary for 24 hours- from 8 a.m. 10th to 8 a.m. 11th June, 1917	11/06/1917	11/06/1917
Miscellaneous	3rd Cavalry Division Intelligence Summary period from 8 a.m. 11th to 8 a.m. 12th June, 1917		
Miscellaneous	3rd Cavalry Division Intelligence Summary for 24 hours- form 8 a.m. 12th to 8 a.m. 13th June, 1917	13/06/1917	13/06/1917
Miscellaneous	3rd Cavalry Division Intelligence Summary for 24 hours- from 8 a.m. 13th to 8 a.m. 14th June, 1917	14/06/1917	14/06/1917
Miscellaneous	3rd Cavalry Division Intelligence Summary for 24 hours-8 a.m. 14th to 8 a.m. 15th June, 1917	15/06/1917	15/06/1917
Miscellaneous	Annexe to 3rd Cavalry Division Intelligence Summary. 14th June, 1917		
Miscellaneous	3rd. Cavalry Division Fortnightly Summary Period ending June, 15th. 1917	15/06/1917	15/06/1917
Miscellaneous	3rd Cavalry Division Intelligence Summary for 24 hours 8 a.m. 15th to 8 a.m. 16th June, 1917.	16/06/1917	16/06/1917
Miscellaneous	3rd Cavalry Division Intelligence Summary for period-8 a.m. 16th to 8 a.m. 17th June, 1917.	17/06/1917	17/06/1917
Miscellaneous	3rd Cavalry Division Intelligence Summary for 24 hours from-8 a.m. 17th to 8 a.m. 18th June, 1917.	18/06/1917	18/06/1917
Miscellaneous	3rd Cavalry Division Intelligence Summary for period-8 a.m. 18th to 8 a.m. 19th June, 1917.	19/06/1917	19/06/1917
Miscellaneous	3rd Cavalry Division Intelligence Summary For 24 Hours, 8 a.m. 19th to 8 a.m. 20th June, 1917.	20/06/1917	20/06/1917
Miscellaneous	3rd Cavalry Division Intelligence Summary for period-8 a.m. 20th to 8 a.m. 21th June, 1917.	21/06/1917	21/06/1917
Miscellaneous	3rd Cavalry Division Intelligence Summary for 24 hours from 8 a.m. 21th to 8 a.m. 22nd June, 1917.	22/06/1917	22/06/1917
Miscellaneous	3rd Cavalry Division Intelligence Summary for period-8 a.m. 22nd to 8 a.m. 23rd June, 1917.	23/06/1917	23/06/1917
Miscellaneous	3rd Cavalry Division Intelligence Summary For 24 Hours 8 a.m. 23rd to 8 a.m. 24th June, 1917.	24/06/1917	24/06/1917
Miscellaneous	Examination of wounded Prisoner of 5th. Company 2nd. R.I.R. who has since deed in Hospital.		
Miscellaneous	Annexe to 3rd. Cavalry Division Intelligence Summary 23rd. June, 1917		
Miscellaneous	Report Of Work For Week Ending 29th. June, 1917	29/06/1917	29/06/1917
Miscellaneous	Report. On New Work for week ending Friday June, 22nd. 1917	22/06/1917	22/06/1917
Miscellaneous	Report Of New Work Week Ending Friday June, 15th. 1917	15/06/1917	15/06/1917

Miscellaneous	Summary of Work Done During Week Ending Friday June-8th. 1917 Appendix 9	08/06/1917	08/06/1917
Miscellaneous	Narrative of Events from May 12th. to May 31st.		
Miscellaneous	3rd Cavalry Division Intelligence Summary from period-8 a.m. 24th to 8 a.m. 25th June, 1917	25/06/1917	25/06/1917
Miscellaneous	3rd Cavalry Division Intelligence Summary For 24 Hours From 8 a.m. 25th to 8 a.m. 26th June, 1917	26/06/1917	26/06/1917
Miscellaneous	3rd Cavalry Division Intelligence Summary For period-8 a.m. 26th to 8 a.m. 27th June, 1917	27/06/1917	27/06/1917
Miscellaneous	3rd Cavalry Division Intelligence Summary For 24 Hour From 8 a.m. 27th to 8 a.m. 28th June, 1917	28/06/1917	28/06/1917
Miscellaneous	3rd Cavalry Division Fortnightly Intelligence Summary, Period ending 8.0. a.m. 30th June, 17	30/06/1917	30/06/1917
Miscellaneous			

1917

appx.1.

GENERAL STAFF
No. G.898/5.

6th. Cav. Bde.	12th. San. Sect.	Chaplain.
7th. Cav. Bde.	C.R.H.A.	Fld. Cashier.
8th. Cav. Bde.	O.C., A.S.C.	Liaison Officer.
3rd. Fd. Sqdn.	A.D.M.S.	Divnl. Gas Officer.
3rd. Sig. Sqdn.	A.D.V.S.	Camp Commandant.
No. 7 L.A.B. Battery.	A.P.M.	A.A. & Q.M.G.
Divnl. Ammn. Col.	D.A.D.O.S.	

---

1. The Division will concentrate on April 5th. in the Area DOUBERS - LEBIEZ - FRESSIN - CAVRON-St-MARTIN - PLUMOISON - MARESQUEL - LESPINOY (all inclusive) in accordance with the attached March Table.

2. The following will move under separate orders which will be issued by the A.A. & Q.M.G.

   (a) Ammunition Park.

   (b) 10th. Reserve Park.

   (c) The dismounted personnel of units.

3. "B" Echelons will accompany their Brigades to the above area.

4. H.A. Batteries (less 'K' Battery) will accompany their Brigades. 'K' Battery will join the 7th. Brigade in the new area in accordance with attached March Table.

5. All sick horses will be evacuated under arrangements to be made by the A.D.V.S. direct with Brigades and Divisional Troops.

6. Divisional Headquarters will move to MARESQUEL - Divisional Report Centre will close at TREPIED at 3 p.m. and reopen at same hour at MARESQUEL.

7. Acknowledge

3rd. April, 1917.

Lieut-Colonel
G.S., 3rd. Cavalry Division.

MARCH TABLE - 3rd. CAVALRY DIVISION.

Unit.	Starting Point.	Time.	Route.	Billeting Area.	Remarks.
6th. Brigade.	Under Brigade arrangements.			PLUMOISON - BOUIN - AUBIN-ST-VAAST - BOUQUEMAISON - CONTES - PETIT-ST-VAAST - ST.VAAST.	The Bde. will close up on its head and be disposed in its new billeting area by 12 noon.
7th. Brigade.	Under Brigade arrangements.	-	Any roads between the VERTON - BOIS-JEAN - LESPINOY road and the ST.JOSSE - SORRUS - ST.JUSTIN - BEAULERIE-ST-MARTIN road (both inclusive)	OFFIN - LOISON - BEAURAINVILLE - LESPINOY - MARENLA - PETIT-BEAURAIN.	(a) Tails of Columns to be East of a North and South line through BOIS-JEAN and MONTREUIL by 12 noon, but no troops must reach BEAURAINVILLE Stn. before 1 p.m. (b) Accomodation for 350 dismounted men must be arranged for in BEAURAINVILLE.
8th. Brigade.	Under Brigade arrangements.	-	Any roads North of the River CANCHE.	GAVRON - ST.MARTIN - WAMBERCOURT - FRESSIN - LEBIEZ - HESMOND - BOUBERS.	(a) The Brigade will be assembled in its new billeting area by 12 noon. (b) The road from OREQUY to LEBIEZ must be kept clear for the passage of the Div. AMMN Coln. and 'K' Battery between 10 a.m. and 11 a.m.

P.T.O.

MARCH TABLE - 3rd. CAVALRY DIVISION.

Unit.	Starting Point.	Time.	Route.	Billeting Area.	Remarks.
3rd. Field Sqdr.	LE-PUITS-BERRAULT.	11-30 a.m.	BOIS-JEAN cross roads pt.80 1000 yards S.E. of BRUNEHAUTPRE.	MARESQUEL.	
Div. H.Q. details 3rd. Sig. Sqdn. In order of march.	Road junction North of the T of TREPIED.	10-30 a.m.	ETAPLES - MONTREUIL Station BRIMEUX.	MARESQUEL. MARESQUEL.	
12th. Sanitary Sn.	To move independently by any roads.			MARESQUEL. MARESQUEL.	Not to reach MARESQUEL before 3 p.m.
L.A.O.Battery. H.Q. IV Bde. R.H.A. "K" Battery. Divnl. Ammn. Col.	VERCHOCQ.	8-30 a.m.	CREQUY - LEBIEZ - B. of BEAURAINVILLE - X roads 500 x West of BEAURAIN CHATEAU.	MARESQUEL. 7th. Bde. Area. BEAURAIN Chateau.	(a) H.Q. R.H.A., "K" Batty and Div. Ammn.Col: to move under orders of O.R.H.A. (b) 7th. Bde. will arrange to meet "K" Batty. at OFFIN and conduct it to billets. (c) Tail of the Div. Ammn.Col: to be clear of the X roads 500 x West of BEAURAIN Chateau by 1 p.m.

6th Cav. Bde.	12th San. Sec.	Field Cashier.
7th Cav. Bde.	O.R.H.A.	Liaison Officer.
8th Cav. Bde.	O.C.A.S.C.	D.W.O.
3rd Fd. Sqdn.	A.D.M.S.	Camp Commandant.
3rd Sig. Sqn.	A.D.V.S.	A.A. & Q.M.G.
Div. Amm. Col.	A.P.M.	
10th Mob. Park.	D.A.D.O.S.	Cav. Corps.) for
	Chaplain.	1st. Cav. Div.) information.

---

1. G.898/11 of 4th. April is cancelled and the following substituted.

2. The Division will march on April 7th. to the Area PREVENT – LIGNY-sur-CANCHE – BOUBERS-sur-CANCHE – MONCHEL – CONCHY-sur-CANCHE – VACQUERIE-le-BOUCQ in accordance with attached March Table.

3. After the heads of columns have passed a North and South line through AUCHY-les-HESDIN – VIEIL-HESDIN – VACQUERIETTE, a distance of 500 yards will be maintained in rear of each Regiment, Battery, and Machine Gun Squadron.

4. B.Echelons and detachments Aux. H.T.Company now with Brigades will move as follows:-
   6th. Cav. Bde. – Join into column in rear of Divnl. Amm.Col. when it passes PLUMOISON.
   7th. Cav. Bde. – Follow Divnl. Amm. Col. until 6th. Cav.Bde. B.Echelon joins column, then follow them.
   8th. Cav. Bde. – Follow their Brigade.
On leaving the PREVENT Area on April 8th. all "B" Echelon and Aux. H.T.Coy. will be Divisionalized, and concentrate at BOUBERS-sur-CANCHE under the orders of the O.C., A.S.C.

5. The Ammunition Park will move on April 7th. under orders to be issued by the A.A. & Q.M.G. When the Division leaves the PREVENT Area it will come under Corps Control.

6. Railhead for 6th. and 7th. will be BOUQUEMAISON.

7. Divisional Headquarters will move to MONCHEL.

8. Acknowledge.

Lieut-Colonel,
G.S., m3rd. Cavalry Division.

5th. April, 1917.

MARCH TABLE - 3rd CAVALRY DIVISION. APRIL 7th.

UNIT.	STARTING POINT.	TIME.	ROUTE.	Billeting Area.	Remarks.
6th Cav. Bde.	X roads at the Church PLUDISON.	9.a.m.	X roads just N. of the A. of Ste.AUSTREBERTHE - WAIL - CONCHY-sur-CANCHE - VACQUERIE-le-BOUCQ.	VACQUERIE-le-BOUCQ - Pt.FORTEL - FORTEL.	
7th. Cav. Bde.	Level crossing BEAURAIN Chateau.	9.15 a.m.	Follow the 6th. Bde.	BOUBERS-sur-CANCHE.	
8th. Cav. Bde.	AICHIN-les-HESDIN STATION.	10.a.m.	Le PARCQ - FRESNOY - WILLEMAN - LINZEUX - FLERS - HAUT-COTE.	FROMENT - LIGNY-sur-CANCHE.	
H.Q. IV Bde.) B.H.A.) 3rd. Fd.Sqdn.) Div.Ammn.Col) in order of march.)	Level crossing Eastern end of MARESQUEL.	10.30 a.m.	Follow the 7th. Bde.	CONCHY-sur-CANCHE. " "	
Div. H.Q. details. 5sd. Sig. Sqdn.	Level crossing eastern end of MARESQUEL.	11a.m.	Follow the Div. Ammn.Col.	MONCHEL.	
10th Res Park.	St. DENOEUX.	9 a.m.	MARESQUEL - HESDIN - WAIL - CONCHY-sur-CANCHE	MONCHEL.	
12th San. Sect.	To move independently.		HESDIN - WAIL.	MONCHEL.	Not to reach MONCHEL before 4 p.m.

MARCH TABLE - 3rd. CAVALRY DIVISION. 8th. April.

Unit.	Starting Point.	Time.	Route.	Billeting Area.	Remarks.
6th. Cav. Bde.	X Roads at N.W. entrance to BONNIERES.	2 p.m.	X roads ARBRE - S. outskirts REBREUVIETTE - IVERGNY - SUS- -St.LEGER - SOMBRIN - FOSSEUX.	FOSSEUX.	
7th. Cav. Bde.	Fm. du BOIS.	2 p.m.	HUMCQ - SERICOURT - MAGNICOURT - AMBRINES - MANIN - NOYELLE - -VIEW-NOYELLETTE - WARLUZEL - X roads S. of Y of SIMENCOURT.	GOUY-en-ARTOIS.	
8th. Cav. Bde.	Forked roads S. of F of FREVENT.	2.40pm.	REBREUVIETTE - LIENCOURT - HAUTEVILLE.	- do -	
H.Q. IV Bde.RHA.	W. exit to	3 p.m.		- do -	
3rd. Fd. Sqdn.	BOUBERS-sur-	3 p.m.			
Div.Ammn.Col.	CANCHE.	3.10p.m	Follow 8th. Cav. Bde.		
"H.Q. details"		3.20p.m			
3rd. Sig.Sqdn.		3.30p.m			
in order of march					
13) 14) Mob.Vet.Sect. 20)	Forked road S. of F in FREVENT.	1.5pm.	Follow 3rd. Signal Sqdn.	- do -	To march under orders to be issued A.D.V.S. Each section will join column in rear of Sig.Sqdn. as latter pass near their area between GOUCHY & FREVENT.
Mot.Res. Park.	W. exit to BOUBERS.	3.30pm.	Follow divisionalized Mob.Vet. Sects to AVESNES-LE-COMTE.	BARLY.	
12th. San.Sect.	To move independently.		Same as 8th. Cav. Bde.	GOUY-en-ARTOIS	Not to reach GOUY before 7 p.m.

app 3.   War Diary

G.896/15.

6th Cav. Bde.	10th Mos. Park.	D.A.D.O.S.
7th Cav. Bde.	12th San. Sec.	Chaplain.
8th Cav. Bde.	C.R.H.A.	Fd. Cashier.
3rd Fd. Sqdn.	O.C.A.S.C.	Camp Commandant.
3rd Sig. Sqn.	A.D.M.S.	A.A. & Q.M.G.
Div. Amm. Col.	A.D.V.S.	Cav. Corps.) for information.
	A.P.M.	1st Cav. Div)

---

1. The Division will march to an area about GOUY-en-ARTOIS on April 8th in accordance with the March Table overleaf.

2. (a) No units will cross the main ST. POL – DOULLENS road before 2.30 p.m.
   (b) A distance of 500 yards will be maintained in rear of each regiment, battery and Machine Gun Squadron.

3. All "B" Echelon Wagons will, so soon as the Division has moved from the FREVENT area, concentrate at BOUBERS-sur-CANCHE under orders which will be issued by the O.C.A.S.C. direct to Brigade Transport Officers and N.C.O's i/c Divisional Troops "B" Echelon.

4. The Ammunition Park will come under Corps control when the Division leaves the FREVENT area.

5. On arrival at the GOUY-en-ARTOIS bivouac, the 6 Q.F. Ammunition Wagons of the Mobile Section Divisional Ammunition Column will join the batteries forthwith and bivouac with them.

6. All Mobile Veterinary Sections will be divisionalized & march under the orders of the A.D.V.S. from the FREVENT area to the GOUY area.

7. Heavy Sections Cavalry Field Ambulances will accompany their Brigades to the GOUY area; on arrival there they will be divisionalized and bivouac under orders which will be issued by the A.D.M.S.

8. All Aux: H.T. Wagons attached to units will concentrate at BOUBERS-sur-CANCHE by 11 a.m. on April 8th.
   Units must make their own arrangements for carrying rugs to the GOUY area.

9. Divisional Headquarters will move to GOUY-en-ARTOIS Chateau.

10. Acknowledge.

Lieut-Colonel.

7/4/17.   G.S. 3rd Cavalry Division.

SECRET

6th Cavalry Bde.	A. P. M.	Cavalry Corps.	For
7th Cavalry Bde.	Div. Amm. Col.	2nd Cav. Division.	
8th Cavalry Bde.	Lieut. A.V. DRUMMOND	17th Division.	infmn.
3rd Field Sqdn.	2nd Life Guards.	37th Division.	
3rd Signal Sqdn.	Capt. C. E. YEATMAN,		
L. A. C. Battery.	1st Life Guards.		
C. R. H. A.	A. A. & Q.M.G.		
A. E. H. S.	Camp Commandant.		
A. D. V. S.			

app 4.

3rd CAVALRY DIVISION CONCENTRATION ORDER No. 1.

1. After Zero +2 hours on "Z" day, the Division will remain Standing-to at one hour's notice. So soon as the first order to move is received, the Division will move into its first position of readiness as follows :-

Forked Roads in L.8c - L.9a s c on the ST POL-ARRAS road.

(a) 8th Brigade will march via the X roads in P.12.a. - WANQUENTIN - BRICKWORKS - GOUVES - DUISANS - X roads in L.2.c. thence along the main ST. POL - ARRAS road to G.13.d.9.4. (Sheet 51B 1/40,000
The Brigade will close up so that its tail is East of the Railway in L.9. *while its head remains at G.13.d.9.4.*

(b) 6th Brigade will follow the 8th Brigade and halt with its head West of DUISANS, and its tail East of GOUVES.

(c) Div. H.Q. details, H.Q., C.R.A., Signal Sqdn., H.Q., Field Sqdn., in order of march will follow the 6th Brigade, halting West of GOUVES.

(d) 7th Brigade will follow the Divisional Troops above mentioned, and halt with its head South of the X roads in K.21.d, tail just East of WANQUENTIN.

(e) "A" Echelons will remain in their Brigade bivouacs, horses harnessed in, but poles down, ready to move at ¼ hour's notice in the order of march of Brigades, A.1. under Lieut. A.V. DRUMMOND, 2nd Life Guards, A.2. under Captain C. YEATMAN, 1st Life Guards.
A.1. will follow the 7th Brigade when it moves forward; A.2. will follow the Divisional Ammunition Column.

(f) Divisional Ammunition Column will remain in its bivouac, same orders as for "A" Echelons, and follow the A.1. Echelon when it moves.

(g) M.V.S's will follow the A.2. Echelon under orders which will be issued by the A.D.V.S.

N.B. (i) All troops will clear the roads and villages as far as possible when halted.

(ii) When any Unit receives the order to move, it will warn the Unit in rear of it.

(iii) So soon as the march is resumed, all Units will close up.

2. at Zero +2 hours ~~at Zero + 1 hour~~ R.E. Field Troops will join their respective Brigades under orders to be issued by O.C., Field Squadron.

3. Batteries will accompany their Brigades.

4. During this Concentration, Divisional Report Centre will be at ~~the North exit of DUISANS.~~ *G.13.d. i.e. at the head of the 8th Bde.*

8th April, 1917.

Lieut.Col.
G.S., 3rd Cavalry Division.

P.T.

appendix 5

SECRET.

3rd. Cavalry Division Concentration Order No.2.

1. The subsequent move forward will take place with a view to bringing the Division into the following position of readiness by the time the infantry attacks are expected to reach the WANCOURT - FEUCHY line, viz at Z + 8 hours.

   (a) 8th. Bde. will move via the ST.POL - ARRAS road to just short of the western exit of ARRAS in G.21.a.4.7. thence due East to the Road Point in G.21.b.5.7. where it will join the Cavalry track "A", which it will follow to the Eastern end of H.31.b.(1/20,000).

   (b) 6th. Bde. will move into the area vacated by the 8th. Bde.

   (c) Divl. Troops and 7th.Bde. will move into the area vacated by the 6th. Bde.

   (d) 'A' Echelon, the Divl. Ammn. Col.and the M.V.S's will move into the area vacated by the 7th. Bde.

   (e) No. 7 L.A.M.Battery will receive separate orders.

2. Divl. Report Centre will move up to the head of the 8th. Brigade. at the Eastern end of H 31 b

3. Subsequent to this concentration, troops will move in accordance with 3rd. Cavalry Division O.O. No.1. issued today.

8th. April, 1917.

Lieut-Colonel,
G.S., 3rd. Cavalry Division.

SECRET.

MEDICAL ARRANGEMENTS for Z day.

(a) All Heavy Sections C.F.A's will remain concentrated at GOUY under the orders of the A.D.M.S..

(b) Pack Mounted Sections will move with Brigades under all circumstances.

(c) Light Sections C.F.A's will be collected so soon as the Division has carried out its first concentration, park just off the road in P.12.a.6.6. and await orders from A.D.M.S.

(d) An advanced Divisional Dressing Station will be established on the main ARRAS - CAMBRAI road about LES-FOSSES-Farm N.11.b.9.4. when the Division moves forward to its first objective.

(e) Divl. Collecting Station for walking cases will be established in the caves in ARRAS where the ARRAS - CAMBRAI road runs into ARRAS.

8th. April, 1917.

A. Paget
Lieut-Colonel,
G.S., 3rd. Cavalry Division.

War Diary app. 6

G. 984

8th. Cavalry Brigade.
7th. Cavalry Brigade.
6th. Cavalry Brigade.
C.R.H.A.
L.A.C. Battery.
3rd. Field Squadron.
3rd. Signal Squadron.

---

1. In the case of a successful advance, flares will be lighted -
    (a) On reaching the first objective.
    (b) At 7 p.m.
    (c) When asked to do so by the aeroplane.

2. The Heavy artillery of the 3rd. and 5th. Army co-operate as follows:-
    The 3rd. Army will bring fire to bear on the villages of -

    FONTAINE-lez-CROISILLES.
    CHERISY.
    HANCOURT.
    REMY.
    VIS-en-ARTOIS.
    BOIRY-NOTRE-DAME.

    The 5th. Army will bring fire to bear on -

    FONTAINE-lez-CROISILLES.
    HENDECOURT.
    CAGNICOURT.

    The fire will be lifted from the above named places when ordered to do so from Cavalry Corps H.Q.

3. No units below Bde. H.Q. will keep any Secret Papers or orders in their possession when they move East of the WANCOURT - FEUCHY line. All maps giving any information of our own distributions should be destroyed.
    Bde. H.Q. should make arrangements to immediately destroy all papers if the necessity to do so should arise.

4. The Divisional Commander holds all unit commanders responsible that every mans waterbottle is full when the units move East.
    Water will not on any account be taken from wells behind the German line until the water has been tested and reported fit to drink by M.O's.

5. In the event of a unit desiring to claim any particular trophy, captured by it, for retention after the war. The unit will act as follows -

    (a) Notify the D.A.D.O.S. of the intention to submit a claim.

    (b) Submit a claim for the article through the usual channel for transmission to Army H.Q.

C.E. Paget
Lieut-Colonel,

8th. April, 1917.   G.S., 3rd. Cavalry Division.

SECRET.
Copy No......75

3rd CAVALRY DIVISION OPERATION ORDER No. 1.

Ref: 51B N.W. & S.W. 1/20,000)
     51B & C.   1/40,000)   April 8th, 1917.

1.   The 3rd Army is attacking the German defences East of ARRAS tomorrow in conjuntion with an attack by the 1st Army on the VIMY RIDGE.
     These attacks will take place at Zero hour which will be notified later.

2.   The 12th and 3rd Divisions of the VIth Corps will attack respectively North and South of the main ARRAS - CAMBRAI road. Their Reserve Brigades will assault the Brown Line (WANCOURT - FEUCHY Line) at approximately Z + 8 hours.
     Should this attack be successful, the 37th Division will pass through the 12th Division and attack MONCHY-le-PREUX and the ground N. & S. of it, between the ARRAS - CAMBRAI Road and the R. SCARPE.

3.   So soon as MONCHY-le-PREUX has been seized, the 3rd Cavalry Division will advance and seize, as its first objective, the line VIS EN ARTOIS - BOIRY NOTRE DAME (both inclusive) protecting its own left flank.
     The 2nd Cavalry Division will, at the same time, advance and seize the line FONTAINE-les-CROISILLES - VIS EN ARTOIS (both exclusive) on the South bank of the R. SENSEE.
     The 50th Infantry Brigade, plus 1 Bde. R.F.A., (17th Divn) will follow the 3rd Cavalry Division in order to relieve it for a further advance.

4.   In consequence the following moves will take place :-

    (a) 8th Brigade will move North of MONCHY-le-PREUX and seize BOIRY-NOTRE-DAME.

    (b) 6th Brigade will move South of MONCHY-le-PREUX AND and seize VIS-en-ARTOIS, gaining touch with the left of the 2nd Cavalry Division (5th Cav. Bde.), and co-operating with that Bde., as well as with the 8th Brigade.
     The first bound will be to the Line ST. ROBART Factory - BOIS de .. VERT - BOIS-de-SART - East end of PELVES.
     Dividing line between Bdes; the MONCHY le PREUX - BOIRY NOTRE DAME road inclusive to the 8th Brigade.

    (c) Divl. Troops and 7th Brigade will follow the 6th Bde. and move into Reserve about H.33 Central.

    (d) A.1. Echelon under Lieut A.V. DRUMMOND, 2nd Life Gds., will follow the 7th Brigade and park in H.32 Central.

    (e) Divl. Amm. Col. will follow A.1. Echelon and park in H.32 Central.

    (f) A.2. Echelon will follow the Div. Amm. Col. and park East of the   track in G.23.c.
        CAVALRY

2.

5. (a) Advanced Divl. Dressing Station will be established on the main ARRAS - CAMBRAI Road about Les FOSSES Farm in H.11.b.4.

    (b) Divisional Collecting Station for walking cases will be established in the Caves in ARRAS where the ARRAS - CAMBRAI Road runs into ARRAS.

6. Advanced Divisional Headquarters will be established in O.7.b.9.6., so soon as the 6th and 8th Brigades have completed the first bound.

A. Paget.
Lieut.-Colonel,
G.S., 3rd Cavalry Division.

8th April, 1917.

Issued 11. a.m.

Copy No		
"	1)	
"	2)	G.S.
"	3	Q.
"	4	A.D.M.S.
"	5	A.P.M.
"	6	6th Cav. Brigade.
"	7	7th Cav. Brigade.
"	8	8th Cav. Brigade.
"	9	C.R.H.A.
"	10	3rd Fd. Squadron.
"	11	3rd Sig. Squadron.
"	12	L.A.M. Battery.
"	13	Cavalry Corps.
"	14	2nd Cavalry Division.
"	15	17th Division.
"	16	37th Division.
"	17	Major H.A. TOMKINSON, R. Dns.
"	18	Major T.C. GURNEY, 2nd L. Gds.
"	19	Major the Marquis of Londonderry. R.H.G.
"	20	Divl. Am. Col.
"	21	Lieut. A.V. DRUMMOND, 2nd L. Gds. i/c A.1. Ech.
"	22	Capt. C.E. YEATMAN, 1st L. Gds. i/c A.2. Ech.
"	23	1st Cavalry Division

through A.G.

Copy No 9.
Appendix 10

SECRET.   G.186.

3rd CAVALRY DIVISION PROVISIONAL DEFENCE SCHEME.

Preliminary Order.

1. It is improbable that the services of this Division will be required unless the enemy make a serious attack, penetrate the GREEN (front) line, and threaten or capture portions of the BROWN (intermediate) Line.

2. The role of the Division in reserve will be to :-

    (a) Counter-attack, or (b) reinforce the troops in the intermediate line.

    For effectively carrying out either task, the main considerations are that all leaders should know the ground well, and that the troops should arrive at their dismounting positions promptly.

3. In consequence, Brigadiers will carry out reconnaissances on 20th instant with their Regimental Officers of lines of approach to dismounting positions E. of VILLERS FAUCON.

4. These routes should be selected as far as possible across country, avoiding roads or villages which would necessitate narrowing the front of the Cavalry, the roads being left free for the R.H.A. and "A" Echelons.

5. Dismounting positions should be selected as far forward as possible consistent with cover and reasonable immunity from shell fire. They should be half-way up a slope, and not just behind a crest or quite at the bottom of a valley, either of which the enemy's artillery might be likely to search.
    So soon as Regiments have dismounted, they will at once move off on foot to positions of readiness previously selected. The led horses will march under the 2nd in Command to the vicinity of the nearest watering place. The O.C., Brigade led horses will keep touch with events and be ready to move according to Brigadiers' orders.

6. The 6th and 7th Brigades will alternately be the Brigade on duty and will be prepared to move at short notice. Exact time will be given later. Order of march;-   6th or 7th Bde, "G" Bty., - 7th or 6th Bde, - 8th Bde.

7. (a) Three limbered wagons per Brigade will be kept packed with ammunition, bombs, Very lights, etc.
    (b) Rations will be carried as under :-
        On man - 1¼ days.
        On horse- Unexpended portion of current day's oats.
        Water bottles will be filled before starting.
    (c) Water carts to be filled and sent to W. exit of VILLERS FAUCON under Brigade arrangements as quickly as possible after the Column has moved.

8. O.C., 7th L.A.M.B. will reconnoitre roads to VILLERS FAUCON and ST. EMILIE.

9. The light Section C.F.A. of Brigade on duty will march to W. exit of VILLERS FAUCON.

-2-

10. Divisional Headquarters will move to BEAU SEJUR, E. 30.

                                                             Major,

17th May, 1917.   G.S., 3rd Cavalry Division.

```
Copy No. 1 to 6th Cavalry Brigade.
 "    "  2 to 7th Cavalry Brigade.
 "    "  3 to 8th Cavalry Brigade.
 "    "  4 to A.A. & Q.M.G.
 "    "  5 to A.D.M.S.
 "    "  6 to Cavalry Corps (for information).
 "    "  7 to 2nd Cav. Div.  (    "         "      ).
```

SECRET.

Copy No 13

G. 186/1.

3rd CAVALRY DIVISION DEFENCE SCHEME.

1. **BOUNDARIES OF DIVISIONAL FRONT.**

    (a) The boundaries of the Divisional Sector which is known as the "D" Sector, are as follows :-

    (i) On South, the line F.8.c.0.0. - N. Side of MAY COPSE - F.6.c.0.2.
    (ii) On North, the line: N. exit of PEIZIERE - TARGELLE Ravine, X.15.d.7.6. - along N. side of Ravine - X.18.a.7.0.

    (b) This area is divided into 2 sub-sectors - the Southern sub-sector being known as D.1., and the Northern as D.2.

    (c) The 2nd Cavalry Division is on our right - the 40th Infy. Division is on our left.

2. **COMMAND.**
    Each sub-sector will be under the command of a Lieut-Colonel, the whole Sector being under a Brigadier-General, whose Headquarters will be at F.1.d.8.8.
    Not more than 2 Lieut-Colonels will be in the line at the same time.

3. **TROOPS ALLOTTED.**
    On taking over from Brig-General BELL-SMYTH's Brigade, troops will be distributed as under :-

    Sub-sector D.1. - 6th Cavalry Brigade.
    -do- D.2. - 7th Cavalry Brigade.

4. **DESCRIPTION OF DEFENCES.**
    There will eventually be 4 lines :-
    (a) The OUTPOST Line.
    (b) The GREEN Line.
    (c) The BROWN Line.
    (d) The BROWN SUPPORT Line.

    (a) consists of a series of posts from the BIRDCAGE in X.29.d.9.8., running northwards to connect with 40th Division about X.17.d.0.7.
    (b) consists of 6 mutually-supporting posts, constructed for all-round defence. They are covered by continuous wire and connected by trenches in places.
    (c) and (d) are partially, but not completely wired. 2 Battalions 178th Infantry Brigade are allotted to 3rd Cavalry Divn., for work on the BROWN Line from 25th to 28th instant. (incl).

5. **METHOD OF HOLDING THE LINE.**
    (a) The OUTPOST and GREEN Lines will be held lightly during the day-time, with plenty of automatic rifles and machine guns and with supports at hand, which can work at night and counter-attack, if necessary, by day or night.
    (b) In order to facilitate reliefs, and to equalise work, the distribution of troops in each sub-sector will be :-
    (i) OUTPOST Line - 1 or 1½ Sqdns., "A" Regiment.
    (ii) GREEN Line. - 3 Sqdns., "B" Regiment.
    (iii) BROWN Line - 3 Sqdns., "C" Regiment.
    The remaining 2 or 1½ Sqdns., of "A" Regiment will be stationed in rear of (ii) or (iii), as accommodation is available.

−2−

6. **DEFENSIVE BARRAGES.**
S.O.S. Lines are arranged for covering both OUTPOST and GREEN Lines. As the number of guns does not admit of a continuous barrage across the whole front, the S.O.S. lines are arranged so as to cover probable lines of approach, and arrangements are made to concentrate quickly on threatened points.

In the event of the OUTPOST Line being captured, the S.O.S. barrage will be brought back to cover the GREEN Line by Artillery Group Commanders in consultation with the Cavalry Brigade Commander.

So soon as possible, O's C. 6th and 7th M.G. Squadrons will inform C' R.H.A. what portion of these barrage lines they can cover with M.G. barrage. This will enable the Artillery barrage to be thicker on the remainder of the line.

7. **PRINCIPLES OF DEFENCE.**
(a) <u>In case of local attacks.</u>
The <u>OUTPOST Line</u> must be held. In the event of the enemy penetrating into any portion of it, he must at once be counter-attacked and ejected.

All Commanders − down to Troop Leaders − must study their positions, and have plans ready for immediate counter-attack with the troops at their disposal at the moment.

(b) <u>In case of attack by the enemy in force.</u>
The <u>GREEN Line</u> is the main line of resistance of the Division and must be held at all costs. Troops holding the OUTPOST Line will do everything possible to delay and break up the enemy's attack. In the event of the enemy penetrating into any portion of the GREEN Line, the commander of the local reserves to that portion will at once counter-attack with the troops immediately available. Should this be unsuccessful, the Brigade Commander will organise a counter-attack <u>at the earliest possible</u> moment, with such of his reserves and of the Artillery at his disposal as may be necessary. If an operation requiring more strength than is at the disposal of the Brigade Commander is necessary, it will be carried out under orders of the Divisional Commander and after such preparation of Field and Heavy Artillery as the circumstances require. Plans for counter-attacks in any of these eventualities will be prepared in advance by the Commanders concerned.

(c) So soon as the Brigadier considers that he is likely to use the Regiment in the BROWN Line, he will inform the Divisional Commander, who will immediately move up the Brigade in training to the BROWN Line.

8. **PATROLLING.**
Instructions have already been issued as to employment of patrols − vide 3rd Cav. Div. No. G.240.

Sub-sector Commanders will submit plans for "fighting patrols" to the Brigadier.

9. **WORK.**
The chief task of the Division will probably consist in working on the defences; this work is classified in order of importance as follows :−

(i) Completion of OUTPOST Line (making continuous, wired trench) from BIRDCAGE to join 40th Division about X.17.d.0.7.
(ii) Completion of posts G.-M. as all-round works.
(iii) Construction of dug-outs for M.G. Detachments, O.P's and Squadron Headquarters'.
(iv) Communications to make movement to and from GREEN Line possible by daylight.

10/

10. CONCEALMENT.
All new work will be screened as far as possible. As camouflage becomes available, approaches will also be screened.

11. RELIEFS.
(i) Lieut-Colonels will be relieved every six days under Brigade arrangements.
(ii) Brigadiers will be relieved every seven days.
(iii) The 8th Cavalry Brigade will relieve the 6th Cavalry Brigade after 9 days.
(iv) The 6th Cavalry Brigade will relieve the 7th Cavalry Brigade after 18 days.

(sd) J. VAUGHAN,
Major-General,
Commanding 3rd Cavalry Division.

21st May, 1917.

SECRET

APPENDIX A.

6th. Cavalry Brigade.
7th. Cavalry Brigade.
8th. Cavalry Brigade.   Cavalry Corps (for information.)
C.R.H.A.   2nd. Cavalry Division. (for information
3rd. Field Squadron.   40th. Division. (for information).
A.D.M.S.

Addendum to 3rd. Cavalry Division Defence Scheme (G.186/1)

Action of Reserve Brigade.
****

1.   One complete Brigade will be in Reserve to the Sector held by the Division(D. Sector) and will remain in back area to continue training as a Brigade.

2.   It is improbable that the services of this Brigade will be required unless the enemy make a serious attack, penetrate the Green line and threaten or capture portions of the Brown Line.

3.   The role of the Brigade in Reserve will be to:-
        (a) counter-attack, or
        (b) reinforce the troops in the Brown line . For effectively carrying out either task, the main considerations are that all Leaders should know the ground well, and that the troops should arrive at their dismounting positions promptly.

4.   In consequence, the Brigadier of Brigade in Reserve will carry out reconnaissances with his Regimental Officers of lines of approach to dismounting positions West and S.W. of EPEHY about squares E.6. E.12.
        These routes should be selected as far as possible across country, avoiding roads or villages which would necessitate narrowing the front of advance, the roads being left free for the R.H.A. and A.Echelons.

5.   Dismounting positions should be selected as far forward as possible consistent with cover and reasonable immunity from shell fire. They should be half-way up a slope, and not just behind a crest or quite at the bottom of a valley, either of which the enemy's artillery might be likely to search.
        So soon as Regiments have dismounted, they will at once move off on foot to positions of readiness previously selected. The led horses will march to a position near water W. of ROISEL.
        The O.C. Brigade led horses will keep touch with events and be ready to move according to Brigadiers orders.

6.   The state of readiness required from Reserve Brigade will be that it shall be ready to move at 4 hours notice from time of receipt of order at Bde. H.Q. Should it appear probable that the services of the Brigade may be required, a warning order will be sent directing Brigade to be ready to move at one hour's notice. 3rd. Signal Squadron will arrange for either telephone or visual signalling communication between Advanced Divl. H.Q. E.22.a.9.6. and H.Q. of Reserve Brigade.

7. (a) Rations will be carried as under:-

   On man - one days iron ration and unexpended portion
            of current days ration.
   On horse - Unexpended portion of current days oats.
   Water bottles will be filled before starting.

   (b) Water carts to be filled and sent to W. exit of
VILLERS FAUCON under Brigade arrangements as quickly as possible
after Brigade has moved.

8. Should Reserve Brigade be short of horses G.O.C.
Reserve Brigade will arrange with nearest Brigade for the loan
of necessary number of horses to complete requirements.

9. Divisional Dump of Ammunition, Bombs, Very Lights, etc.,
is being formed at E.16.c.3.1.
   Should more ammunition be required than is carried on
the men this will be obtained from Divisional Dump.

23rd. May, 1917.

Major,
G.S., 3rd. Cavalry Division.

ORDERS FOR RELIEF.

1. The 3rd. Cavalry Division will take over the Sector of trenches now held by BELL SMYTH'S Brigade of 2nd. Cavalry Division. Relief to be completed by dawn on 25th. May.

2. 8th. Cavalry Brigade will remain in their present area for training.

3. The Group of artillery allotted to the Division consists of the following units which will be under the command of Lt.Col WAINEWRIGHT Commanding IV Brigade R.H.A..
4th. Brigade R.H.A. (less Battery of Brigade training).

    B/296 Battery R.F.A.
    C/296   "   R.F.A.
    D/296   "   R.F.A.

Brigade Staff of 296th. Brigade R.F.A. will be withdrawn on completion of re-grouping.

4. A.D.M.S. will arrange direct with A.D.M.S. 2nd. Cav. Div. regarding relief of medical units now in BELL SMYTH'S Brigade Sector.
 (a) A Regimental Aid Post will be established at Regtl. H.Q. of Lt.Cols. Commanding D.1 and D.2 sub-sectors.
 (b) There will also be an aid post in EPEHY, exact position of which will be notified later.
Details regarding reliefs will be notified to Brigades by A.D.M.S.
 (c) There will be a combined 2nd. and 3rd. Cav. Div. Main Dressing Station in VILLERS FAUCON.

5. Two Battalions 178th. Inf. Bde. now in Reserve to 2nd. Cav. Div. *[will be allotted to 3rd Cav: Div]* for wiring work on the Intermediate line from the 25th. to 28th. inst. (inclusive). Orders regarding their movements will be issued later.

6. Arrangements for the transfer of Signal personnel are being made by A.D.Signals.

7. 3rd. Field Squadron which is now working in BELL SMYTH's Brigade Area, will remain there when relief takes place, and will come under orders of 3rd. Cav. Division.

8. The Sector to be taken over by the 3rd. Cav. Div. from BELL SMYTH'S Brigade is called D. Sector and id divided into two sub-sectors numbered D.1 and D.2 from Right to Left.
BELL SMYTH'S Brigade consists of 3rd. Cav. Bde. together with 2nd. Dragoons (R.S.Greys) of 5th. Cav. Bde.

9. Brig-Gen. A.E.W.HARMAN D.S.O. with H.Q. 6th. Cav. Bde. will take over Command from Brig-Gen. J.A.BELL SMYTH C.M.G. on night 24th/25th. and the relief will be carried out as under:-
 6th. Cav. Bde. will take over sub-sector D.1 now held by 4th. Hussars in front line and 16th. Lancers in support.
 7th. Cav. Bde. will take over sub-sector D.2 now held by R.S.Greys in front line with 5th. Lancers in support.
 Each Brigade sub-sector will be commanded by a Lieut-Col. with Regtl. Staff; the remaining regiments of the Brigade being commanded by 2nd. in command or a senior Squadron Leader. Dismounted Establishments have been notified to all units concerned.

10. Details of relief are as under:-

Night 23rd/24th.

(a) All machine guns of BELL SMYTH'S Brigade and 4 M.Gs. of 5th. M.G. Squadron will be relieved by 6th. and 7th. M.G. Sqdns. in their respective sub-sectors.

(b) 4 Squadrons each from 6th. and 7th. Brigades will relieve 16th. Lancers and 5th. Lancers respectively in and about Brown Line.

11. **Night 24th/25th.**

4 Squadrons each from 6th. and 7th. Brigades in and about Brown Line will relieve 4th. Hussars and R.S. Greys respectively in Outpost and Green Lines.

Remainder of 6th. and 7th. Brigades will take place of above 8 Squadrons in and about Brown Line.

12. All units of 3rd. Cav. Div. will come under the orders of G.O.C. BELL SMYTH'S Brigade until command passes to Brig-Gen. HARMAN on completion of reliefs on night 24th/25th.

13. All units will move mounted to a position already reconnoitred East of SAULCOURT about E.11, when horses will be sent back immediately to permanent bivouacs. Troops will not reach neighbourhood of EPEHY before 8.30 p.m. and will not move in large bodies.

14. Further details affecting relief have been communicated direct to 6th. and 7th. Brigades (G.244).

15. Orders regarding Divisional Staff Officers for Advanced Divisional H.Q. will be notified later.

16. Advanced Divisional H.Q. will open at E.22.a.9.6. N.W. of VILLERS FAUCON at 5 p.m. on 24th. May.

Command of D. Sector will pass from G.O.C. 2nd. Cav. Div. to G.O.C. 3rd. Cav. Div. at 9 a.m. on 25th. May.

Major,

22nd. May, 1917.   G.S., 3rd. Cavalry Division.

Copies to:-

6th. Cav. Bde.
7th. Cav. Bde.
8th. Cav. Bde.
3rd. Field Sqdn.   Field Cashier.
3rd. Sig. Sqdn.   French Liaison Officer.
L.A.M. Battery.   Chaplain.
Amm. Col.   A.A. & Q.M.G.
A.D.M.S.   Camp Commandant.
A.D.V.S.   ---------
Supply Col.
A.P.M.   Cavalry Corps (for information).
O.C. A.S.C.   2nd. Cav. Div. (for information.)
D.A.D.O.S.   Brig-Gen Bell Smyth's Bde. (for informatio

Appendix 12

GENERAL STAFF,
3RD
CAVALRY DIVISION.
G. 244.

6th. Cav. Bde.
7th. Cav. Bde.
8th. Cav. Bde.
A.D.M.S.
A.A. & Q.M.G.
BELL SMYTH's Bde. (for information.).

----

1. The following detailed arrangements made with BELL SMYTH'S Brigade and notified verbally to Brigade Majors 6th., 7th., and 8th. Brigades on night 21st. are issued in confirmation thereof.

2. Should any alteration be required, Brigades will arrange direct with BELL SMYTH'S Brigade.

3. Night 22nd/23rd. May.

    6th. and 7th. M.G. Squadrons:- 3 officers from each M.G. Squadron will report at H.Q. BELL SMYTH'S Brigade (F.1.d.8.8.) at 8 p.m. on 22nd. They will be met by guides and shown all M.G. emplacements.

4. Night 23rd/24th. May.

    6th. and 7th. M.G. Squadrons:- Will relieve the 12 M.Gs of 3rd. M.G. Squadron now in and about GREEN Line. Arrangements for relief will be made between officers sent on in advance on night 22nd/23rd. and O.C. 3rd. M.G. Squadron. Relief not to commence before 9 p.m. from cross-roads in EPEHY (F.1.c.9.8.).
Note.
(3rd. M.G. Squadron now use 3 L.G.S. Wagons every night for carrying water, rations, material etc., up to their posts).

    6th. Cav. Bde in D.1. Sector.) will each send up four
    7th. Cav. Bde in D.2 Sector.)
dismounted Squadrons to relieve 16th. Lancers (3 Sqdns) and 5th. Lancers (3 Sqdns) who each have one Sqdn. in support to GREEN Line and two in and about BROWN LINE. Representatives from these Squadrons will go forward to reconnoitre Outpost line and GREEN Line.

    Guides for these Squadrons and for those officers and N.C.Os going to front line will be at Reserve Battalion H.Q. or respective Sectors at 9.15 p.m. These H.Q. are situated in EPEHY at F.1.c.6.5. and W.30.d.8.1.

    The Squadron moving into support of GREEN Line will come under the orders of Os.C. 4th. Hussars and R.S. Greys respectively.

    Signallers, will be sent on to reconnoitre existing lines.

5. Night 24th/25th.

    6th. Cav. Bde. in D.1. Sector.) The four Squadrons sent on
    7th. Cav. Bde. in D.2. Sector.)
in advance will take ove Outpost Line, GREEN Line and the 1 Squadron in Support to GREEN Line; under arrangements made by them direct with Lt-Cols. Comdg. sub-sectors, relieving 4th. Hussars and R.S. Greys whose H.Q. are in F.3.b.8.5. and X.26.c.4.6.

    Remainder of 6th. and 7th. Brigdes will move into neighbourhood of BROWN Line, taking over the positions held on previous night by their own Squadrons, under Brigade arrangements.

    Brigade H.Q. 6th. Cav. Bde. will relieve Bde. H.Q. 3rd. Cav. Bde.

    Note. BELL SMYTH'S Brigade will hand over all maps, pland etc, affecting their Sector.

6. Dumps etc., are as shown on attached plan.

22/5/17.

                        Sd. E. de Burgh, Major,
                        3rd. Cavalry Division.

Appendix 24

3rd. Cavalry Division Summary of Intelligence 11 a.m.
24th. - to 11 a.m. 25th. May 1917.
==*=*=*=*

1. OPERATIONS on Divisional Front.

   (a) Patrols.
   Patrols report enemy working all night in the vicinity of CANAL WOOD.
   (b) Our Artillery.
   Our guns shelled S.10.c.4.2. where men were seen walking about in two's and three's.

2. Hostile attitude and activity.

   (a) Artillery - Several gas shells fell into EPEHY during the night.
   (b) Movements.- At 11 a.m. 24th. 30 men were seen drilling at T.22.c. (Ground observation).
   Thirty horses were seen grazing just N. of BEAUREVOIR at 4.25 p.m. 24th.
   (c) Aviation. - only two enemy aeroplanes crossed our lines.

3. Hostile Defences.

   (a) Work and new trenches.
   Small parties were seen working on the trenches in the HINDENBURG LINE.
   (b) Demolitions.
   Clouds of smoke were seen rising from BANTOUZELLE in M.26.d. at 11 a.m. yesterday.

4. Miscellaneous.

   Our aeroplanes have shown great activity to-day. The enemy's Anti-aircraft Guns have been very busy but without any success.

                              Sd. W.P.Browne, Captain,
                              General Staff,
                              3rd. Cavalry Division.

25th. May, 1917.

3rd. Cavalry Division Intelligence Summary from 11 a.m.
25/5/17 to 11 a.m. 26/5/1917.

1. OPERATIONS on Divisional Front.

    (a) Patrols.

    Patrols to CANAL WOOD during the night, encountered no opposition.

    (b) Artillery.

    At 12 noon our artillery shelled an enemy working party in S.10.c.1.9.
    38 rounds were fired by our 18 pdrs. on the enemy dugouts in S.9.c.2.3.

2. Hostile Attitude and Activity.

    (a) Artillery.

    No. 7 post (N.W. of OSSUS WOOD) and M. redoubt were shelled yesterday afternoon.
    LITTLE PRIEL FARM was shelled at intervals during the day and night, from the direction of OSSUS.
    X.22.c. was shelled frequently during the day, by a 4.2
    (b) Movement.
    At 8 a.m. single men and small parties were seen moving from S.9.c. to LA TERRIERE.
    Observation balloon ascended and decended at GUISANCOURT FARM T.27.c.
    2 horse-drawn wagons were seen going eastwards in B.9.a.
    Horses were seen grazing in T.28.d.
    (c) Aviation.
    At 6 p.m. 6 hostile machines crossed our lines W. of HONNECOURT WOOD.

3. Hostile Defences.
    (a) During yesterday evening trench mortars were active against the BIRDCAGE. A machine gun was located last night at X.23.d.7.2. It was subsequently moved to X.29.b.7.8. and was observed to fire from there.
    (b) Demolitions.
    At 1.30 p.m. a fire was observed to be burning in BANTOUZELLE
    About 12.15 p.m. a large explosion was observed in LA TERIERE

4. Hostile Organisation.
    (a) Dumps.
    There is evidence of a dump about S.19.d.0.5., wagons being seen to stop there.

5. Miscellaneous.
    (a) Enemy Searchlight.
    At 11 p.m. an enemy searchlight from the direction of LA TERRIERE was directed on an aeroplane which was flying over PEIZIERE.
    (b) Suspected Booby Trap.
    In the Quarry X.23.a. there is a piece of string with a button on the end joining on to a piece of wire which leads into a heap of rubble near the outpost H.Q. Dug-outs.

Sd. W.P.Browne, Captain,
General Staff,
26th. May, 1917.   G.S., 3rd. Cavalry Division.

3rd Cavalry Division Intelligence Summary

from 11 a.m. 26/5/1917 to 11 a.m. 27/5/1917.

1. **OPERATIONS ON DIVISIONAL FRONT.**
    (a) **Our patrols.**
     1. An Officer and two men entered OSSUS WOOD during the night. They report short lengths of trench round the edge of the wood, and could hear Germans talking, but could not see them.
     2. A patrol was sent out from a post in X.23 and report enemy in trench at X.29.a.0.1. Further details not yet received.
     3. The patrol which went to CANAL WOOD on the night 25/26th found the N. and W. edges of the wood wired.

    (b) **Artillery.**
     Our guns fired, (with balloon observation), during the day on VENDHUILLE Quarry in S.14.d., where some Infantry bivouacs were suspected.
     We also fired on CANAL WOOD (with balloon observation) at 6-12 a.m. "K" Battery directed punishment fire (in reply to trench mortar activity on the enemy's trenches in X.30.a.8.3.

2. **HOSTILE ATTITUDE AND ACTIVITY.**
    (a) **Artillery.**
     The works S. of PETIT PRIEL FARM were shelled intermittently during the day and night from the direction of OSSUS. Several H.E. shells fell in X.23.
     One of our posts was shelled this morning with H.E., after the garrison had been withdrawn.
     In the Sector on our right, the Germans put 160 4·2's into LEMPIRE yesterday afternoon, in section salvoes. This area was also shelled intermittently by 77 mm Field Guns.
    (c) **Aviation.**
     At 3-40 p.m. one of our aeroplanes was brought down under control about X.8.d. Central. The enemy shelled it on the ground.
     At 5-15 p.m. five enemy machines crossed our lines, but withdrew again in a S.E. direction under the fire of our A.A. guns.

3. **HOSTILE DEFENCES.**
    M.G's and T.M's
     (i) The trench mortars in OSSUS WOOD were again active against the BIRDCAGE and Quarry (X.29.d.22.), at intervals between 9 p.m. and 12 midnight, and again at 6 a.m.
     (ii) At 10-40 p.m., several M.G. bullets from direction of OSSUS came over X.22.c.4.0.

4. **Miscellaneous.**
     One Division of this Corps carried out a most successful raid last night in the neighbourhood of BELLENGLISE. They captured 18 prisoners (3 wounded) and killed 11 Germans, our casualties being 2 wounded. Prisoners belong to 164th Regt (10th 11th Companies).

27th May, 1917.

(Sd) W.P. BROWNE,
Captain,
G.S., 3rd Cavalry Division.

3rd. Cavalry Division Intelligence Summary from 8 a.m.

27th. to 8 a.m. 28th. May, 1917.

1. Operations on Divisional Front.

(a) Our artillery.

At 2 p.m. our field guns shelled the Quarry in S.14.a.3.8. where enemy movement was observed.

At 4 p.m. our field guns directed punishment fire against the W, end of VENDHUILE, causing an explosion there — probably a small ammunition dump.

At 11.30 p.m. we fired on transport, which was heard to be moving on the road from X.30. to OSSUS.

(b) Our snipers.

At dawn on 27th. 4 men were observed to enter OSSUS WOOD. Snipers claim to have hit two.

(c) Hostile bombing patrol.

At 2.30 a.m. a party of 8 Germans, with bombs, attempted to attack the communication trench between the QUARRIES and the BIRDCAGE. They came from OSSUS WOOD. They were fired on by a Hotchkiss Rifle from the communication trench and fled back to the wood, dropping a rifle, 7 bombs and a cap. They were followed for some distance but they did not appear to have suffered any casualties.

2. Hostile attitude and activity.
(a) Artillery.
(i) Between 3.30 and 4 p.m. the enemy fired 20 rounds (77 mm. shell) at our trenches in X.22.c.
(ii) At 11 a.m. the enemy searched with shrapnel, ground between X.17.a. central and X.17.c.central. This area was again shelled at 2.45 p.m. The direction of the gun appeared to be RANCOURT FARM.
(iii) LITTLE PRIEL FARM was shelled at intervals during the day.
(b) Movement.
(i) Yesterday morning, movement was seen in the enemy's trenches N. of HARGIVAL FARM.
(ii) An A.A. gun was seen about M.35.a. at 10 a.m. yesterday. It moved away again at 11.30 a.m.
(iii) At 6 a.m. today, 3 transport wagons came from M.35.a.9.9. and disappeared behind the wood at M.36.a.5.1.
(iv) Between 7.35 a.m. and 7.50 a.m., several small parties of the enemy were seen moving on this road i.e. from M.35.a.9.9. to M.36.a.5.1.

Considerable movement was heard on the road from X.30.central into OSSUS, which may confirm the report of a dump in OSSUS (see 3rd. Cav. Div. Summary 26/5/17 para. 4 a.).
(c) Aviation.
5.30 a.m. 28th. 1 hostile plane flew over our lines in X.23. and 29 and disappeared southwards.

6.45 a.m. 28th. 1 enemy machine manoeuvred over our lines for 25 minutes, flying over VILLERS GUISLAINS and then in S.E. direction and finally returning towards LA TERRIERE.

3. Hostile Defences.
(a) M.G's and T.M's.
A hostile M.G. fired at one of our aeroplanes over X.23, 29, from the direction of OSSUS WOOD. This fire was returned by our machine.

At

At 11.30 p.m. bullets from an enemy M.G. passed over X.22.c.4.8. from the direction of OSSUS WOOD.

3 enemy M.G's are suspected in OSSUS WOOD one on N. edge of of wood, 100x from W. extremity.

2 black openings on a bank about S.10.c.5.5. were spotted as possible M.G. emplacements.

4. The following enemy movements for 24 hours ending 8 a.m. 27th. were not reported in yesterday's Summary:-

(a) 10.40 a.m. 26th. 4 Germans seen working, as if laying a telephone wire, about S.9.b.central. They were afterwards seen with some papers (or maps) at S.9.d.5.3.

(b) 11.45 a.m. 26th. 12 men walked from S.9.b.central to LA TERRIERE.

(c) At 1.9 p.m. 26th. a working party of 20 men collected S. of the Farm at T.20.b.9.9. and were seen to walk towards the Farm.

                                                  Sd. W.P.Browne, Capt,
                                                      General Staff,

28th. May, 1917.   G.S., 3rd. Cavalry Division.

3rd. Cavalry Division Intelligence Summary from 8 a.m.
28th to 8 a.m. 29th. May, 1917.

1. Operations on Divisional Front.
   (a) Patrols.
       (i) A patrol from G.Post reported a large enemy wiring party on the KNOLL. This patrol found 2 barricades on the road at F.5.d.8.4., manned by 2 Germans with what appeared to be a machine gun.
       (ii) Reconnaissance of OSSUS WOOD.
       A patrol, of 1 Officer and 6 men, entered the West corner of OSSUS WOOD at 4 a.m. They found some holes dug along the inside edge of the Wood and a shed, which may provide cover for sentry groups by night.
       They went on, inside the S. edge of the Wood and encountered no obstacles until they reached X.30.a.1.7. Here, they found a barricade of felled trees and French wire. They, also, heard voices, which appeared to come from an entrenched position about 10^x beyond, on the edge of the Wood.
       This line ran straight across the wood. There is a strong wire entanglement across the road, which runs along the N. edge of the wood. (This road is really about 20^x inside the Wood and not outside, as shown on the map).
       The undergrowth was very thick and nothing could be seen of the men, whose voices were heard. The officer does not think that the line was strongly held.
   (b) Our artillery.
       At 2.30 p.m. we put 26 rounds of shrapnel into CANAL WOOD.
       Between 3.30 p.m. and 4.30 p.m. we shelled LA TERRIERE with good effect.

2. Hostile Attitude and Activity.
   (a) Artillery.
       Our trenches in X.23.c. and X.29.a. were shelled at 9.30 a.m. from beyond BONY, at very long range.
       All our trenches in X.23 received some attention from the enemy's artillery.
       Of 8 enemy shells, which were fired into X.28.d. at 4.45 p.m., 7 were DUDS.
   (b) Movement.
       At 11.25 a.m. a man was seen laying a telephone wire from S.9.d.9.3. into LA TERRIERE at S.15.b.6.9.
       The usual amount of movement was observed in the HINDENBURG LINE S. of LA TERRIERE.
       At 6.55 a.m. today, considerable movement of small parties was seen in M.33.b.
   (c) Aviation.
       At 4.4 p.m. a hostile observation balloon ascended from a point N. of VAUCELLES WOOD and descended at 4.40 p.m.
       At 7.55 p.m. 2 enemy machines flew along our lines.

3. Hostile Defences.
   (a))
   (b)) vide para. 1 (a) (ii) above.

   (c) A.A. Guns and M.Gs.
       The A.A.Gun which is reported to be at M.16.c.9.4. appears to have a bright red body and a dark yellow barrel.
       There is believed to be an A.A. Gun in the Wood at S.8.d.
       The OSSUS WOOD machine guns were again active, day and night.

(d)

(d) <u>Demolitions</u>.

At 12.40 p.m. a large fire was observed at AUBENCHEUL, which was apparently extinguished about 1 p.m.

4. <u>Miscellaneous</u>.

"Periscope Tree", near QUENNEMONT Farm, has been removed.

5. <u>Information from the Division on our Left</u>.

(i) There is a suspected O.P. in RANCOURT FARM - A man was seen observing from a window there.

(ii) On the Afternoon of the 26th. a hostile aeroplane flying very high, crossed our lines firing a machine gun, apparently at no particular target. It appeared to be marked with black and white lines as shewn below.

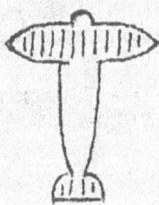

29th. May, 1917.

Sd. W.P.Browne, Captain,
General Staff,
3rd. Cavalry Division.

3rd. Cavalry Division Intelligence Summary for 24 hours -

8 a.m. 29th. to 8 a.m. 30th. May, 1917.

1. Operations in Divisional Front.

   (a) Patrols.
   A patrol was again sent to the Willow Trees at F.5.d.8.4. The barricade reported in yesterday's Summary (para 1 a.(i)) on the VENDHUILLE - TOMBOIS FARM road, proves to be the junction of a trench running N. and S. and not an isolated barrier.
   A small trench is just W. of the Willows and is entirely surrounded by wire. This trench was unoccupied.
   A patrol to CANAL WOOD reported no movement there.
   (b) Enemy patrol.
   At 10.15 p.m. a hostile patrol was fired on in F.6.a. by a M.G. in our outpost line. They withdrew at once.
   (c) Our machine guns.
   From 9.30 p.m. to 1 a.m., our machine guns carried out a shoot on suspected dumps etc.

2. (a) Hostile Attitude and Activity.
   (a) Artillery.
   The BIRDCAGE and QUARRY were shelled intermittently yesterday morning.
   At 12.50 p.m. LITTLE PRIEL FARM was shelled with 77mm's and the BIRDCAGE with 4.2's - about 40 rounds being fired.
   (b) Movement.
   An unusual amount of transport was seen on the GOUY - BEAUREVOIR Road.
   3 wagons were seen on the main road near RANCOURT FARM.
   At 10 a.m., a man was seen to emerge from an isolated tree about S.9.a.5.4.; he disappeared into the wood in S.8.d.
   At 1.15 p.m., 8 men were seen walking on the road in T.21.d. They turned Eastwards to PETIT VERGER FARM.
   At 8.0.a.m., 2 men were seen to get into a trench about S.14.d.2½.7.

   (c) Aviation.
   (i) Between 5.45 p.m. and 6 p.m., 2 hostile aeroplanes flew over our lines but made off in a N.E. direction, on being fired at by our guns.
   (ii) At 7.30 p.m. one enemy machine manoeuvred over our lines for 10 minutes but was driven off by our A.A. Guns.
   (iii) At 7.50 p.m. 2 machines flew over our lines, going North.
   (iv) At 8.30 p.m. One hostile aeroplane flew over PETIT PRIEL FARM and came under fire from our A.A. Guns. He made off East but is reported to have come down in a spiral underneath the balloon which appears to be about T.25.
   (v) 7.15 p.m. - 8 p.m. an aeroplane, spotting for enemy's artillery, manoeuvred over our lines, towards EPEHY. It was painted underneath in black and yellow stripes.
   (vi) 6.30 a.m. 30th. 2 enemy machines circled over VILLERS GUISLAINS and disappeared is a Westerly direction.

3. Hostile Defences.
   Suspected M.G. emplacement.
   Artillery Observation reports a suspected M.G. emplacement at F.6.a.3½.9.

4. Hostile Organisation.

Communications.

At 10.a.m. 29th. 3 Germans were seen working on a new air-line on the road at M.36.a.5.1.

5. General.

Attention is drawn to the unusual activity shown by the enemy's airmen.

The machine reported in 2 c (vi) above, appears to have been similar to that reported in yesterday's Summary para 5 (seen over the sector on our left.)

           Sd. W.P. Browne, Captain,
           General Staff,
30th. May, 1917.   3rd. Cavalry Division.

3rd CAVALRY DIVISION SUMMARY OF INTELLIGENCE FOR

24 hours - 8 a.m. 30th to 8 a.m. 31st May, 1917.

1. OPERATIONS ON DIVISIONAL FRONT.
   (a) *Patrols.*
   An Officer patrol went out, on the night 29/30th, from the S.E. corner of the BIRDCAGE. They were discovered by a party of 6 or 8 Germans, out in front of the enemy's wire (presumably a listening post or protective patrol). The latter promptly retired behind their own wire and put up several flares. Our patrol was unable to proceed further.
   (b) *Our Machine Guns.*
   Between 11-30 p.m. and 1-30 a.m., our M.G.'s fired on OSSUS WOOD, the R.E. Dump at OSSUS and the exits of VENDHUILLE.
   (c) *Our Snipers.*
   An Officer, who was "sniping" on the right of our Sector, located an enemy sniper in a tree at X.29.b.5.6. (OSSUS WOOD). At 7-0 p.m. the Officer got a good shot at the German, who was seen to fall.

2. HOSTILE ATTITUDE AND ACTIVITY.
   (a) *Enemy's Artillery.*
   (i) LEMPIRE and RONSSOY came in for the usual intermittent shelling - at 5-0 p.m. the enemy fired 60 5.9s into RONSSOY and BASSE BOULOGNE, from the direction of BELLICOURT.
   (ii) LITTLE PRIEL FARM was shelled from the direction of VENDHUILLE.
   (iii) 6 H.E. Shells fell into PIGEON RAVINE, about 6-30 p.m.
   (b) *Movement.*
   8-10 a.m. 4 men were seen at X Roads S.13.a. They were dispersed by our Artillery.
   9-0 a.m. 2 Germans were seen to walk from the ruin at S.20.d.8.6. to a small earthwork at S.20.b.1.3.
   11-15 a.m. A party of Cavalry were seen on the LORMISSET - BEAUREVOIR Road.
   11-15 a.m. A motor cyclist entered GUISANCOURT FARM T.27.c.2.5.
   11-47 a.m. A party of 25 Germans were seen on the road - A.4.a.3.4. - One of our forward guns engaged them and the first shell was clearly seen to cause casualties.
   2-15 p.m. A party of 20 men were seen working on a trench about T.22.c.8.9.
   (c) *Aviation.*
   4-25 p.m. 2 hostile planes appeared over VILLERS GUISLAINS and flew a short way along our lines, disappearing in a S.E. direction.
   6-10 p.m. 2 enemy machines came over.
   6-20 p.m. 1 " " came from the S.E., but was driven off by our A.A. Guns.

3. HOSTILE DEFENCES.
   (a) *Enemy work and wire.*
   A reconnaissance of CANAL WOOD revealed the following details:-
   The enemy's wire runs along the W. side of the Wood at the N.W. extremity; it is 20^x from the Wood and it slants back into the Wood at the S.W. corner. There are no trenches W. of the Wood.
   (b) *M.G's and T.M's.*
   M.G. fire against our trench in X.23.a.9.9. had been active during the night 29/30th and continued during the day (30th). The fire appeared to come from the vicinity of BOSQUET FARM.-X.18.a.
   (c) Enemy snipers reported active in W. end of OSSUS WOOD.

4. MISCELLANEOUS.
(i) One of our Batteries was shelled with 8" shells at 7-30 p.m. on the 29th - about 8 rounds being fired. The shelling then ceased, and a hostile aeroplane flew close over the position and appeared to be taking photographs.
The enemy appeared to be ranging by balloon observation. The shells are reported to have been fired from A.18.c.9.9. (our balloons).
(ii) The Division on our left report M.G.s located at X.11.d.3.7. and X.18.a.6.8.

GENERAL NEWS.
The total number of prisoners and guns captured by the Italians since 14th instant is :-
23,691 prisoners (including 604 Officers).
36 guns (13 of heavy calibre)
148 M.G.s
27 T.M.s

LATE NEWS.
An Officer's patrol went to OSSUS WOOD last night. They were fired on by a sniper in a tree. One of the Officers crept forward and fired at the sniper, who was then seen to be hanging from a bough. The Officer fired again and the man crashed to the ground.
Further reconnaissance had by then become impossible, the garrison having been aroused.

(sd) W.P. BROWNE,
Captain,
G.S., 3rd Cavalry Division.

31st May, 1917.

3rd CAVALRY DIVISION FORTNIGHTLY SUMMARY,

Period ending 31st May, 1917.

1. PRISONERS.
No prisoners have been captured yet.

2. OPERATIONS.
(a) General.
The enemy's attitude has been a defensive one.
The only occasions, on which enemy parties of more than 4 men approached our lines, were as follows :-
(i) On the night 27/28th at 2-30 a.m. a party of 8 Germans, armed with bombs, attempted to attack the communication trench between the QUARRY and the BIRDCAGE. The enemy came out of OSSUS WOOD. They appear to have reached the edge of this communication trench, when one of our Hotchkiss Rifles opened fire on them. They fled back to the Wood, dropping a rifle, seven bombs and a cap. They were promptly followed up, but no sign of any casualties could be seen.
(ii) On the night 29/30th about 9-40 p.m., 20 men left the German trenches about F.6.a.4.9. They found our post on the alert and withdrew on being fired at.

3. AIR ACTIVITY.
(a) The enemy has shewn little enterprise in the air. Normally, not more than 2 or 3 aeroplanes fly over our trenches daily, and it is very rare for an enemy machine to pass the line LEMPIRE - EPEHY.
(b) The enemy has not carried out any bombing raids behind our part of the line.

4. ENEMY WORKS.
(a) The enemy appears to be working more on his defences East of the CANAL, than on his outpost positions. His chief centre of activity has lately been in rear of the HINDENBURG Line, about BEAUREVOIR. It is, however, far more difficult to observe the enemy's movements W. of the CANAL than E. of it. The only enemy work that appears to be newly constructed is at the Farm in T.20.b.9.9., where our O.P. reports a suspected gun emplacement.
(b) Considerable traffic is observed on the following roads :-
(i) The BEAUREVOIR - GOUY Road, about BELLEVUE Farm.
(ii) The BEAUREVOIR - VILLERS OUTREAUX Road, about T.27.b.
(c) Patrols have found the enemy's outpost positions in CANAL WOOD and OSSUS WOOD well wired.

[signature]
Captain,
G.S., 3rd Cavalry Division.

31st May, 1917.

3rd. Cavalry Division Intelligence Summary for 24 hours

from 8 a.m. 31st. May, to 8 a.m. 1st. June 1917.

1 Operations on Divisional Front.

(a) Our patrols.

(i) On the evening of 30th/31st. a patrol with 2 officers was sent towards OSSUS WOOD in order to cover the relief of the BIRDCAGE from that direction. The intention was to get close up under the S. edge of the wood before the enemy put out his night outposts and to lie in wait there for patrols leaving the wood. The party was delayed by a sniper in a tree until 7.30 p.m. when one of the officers shot him. When they were 100 yards from the wood an automatic rifle opened fire and Very lights were sent up all along the edge of the wood. The party remained in observation until the relief had been completed. (vide late news in yesterday's Summary).

(ii) A patrol consisting of 1 Sergeant and 8 men went out during the night 31st/1st. from G work to the willow trees at F.5.d. They passed through three lots of wire but report no sign of the enemy. The patrol left at 10.30 p.m. and returned at 1.15 a.m.

(iii) During the night a party of Germans with a M.G. patrolled the Copse just W. of CANAL WOOD.

(b) Our artillery.
Our guns shelled VENDHUILE and CANAL WOOD during the day.

2. Hostile attitude and activity.

(a) Artillery.
PETIT PRIEL FARM was shelled at intervals during the day and night. An old German O.P. has been found in the farm.

Between 10.45 a.m. and 11.25 a.m. the enemy shelled the Quarry at X.17.c. with 5.9's.

At 5.30 p.m. the enemy fired 50 77 mm shells into X.29.a., from the direction of OSSUS.

(b) Movement.
9.15 a.m. A working party was seen in S.22.b.
11.45 a.m. Man carrying two camp kettles left trench on road side at S.3.b.1.4. and disappeared S.4.a.3.3.
3 p.m. A party was seen carrying planks into VENDHUILE.
5.30 p.m. Two men were seen to leave small pit S.14.a.central.
A tripod supporting a white flag was seen at S.14.a.4.9.
a white flag was also seen at S.15.c.3.1.

(c) Aviation.
4 enemy machines were seen, none of which crossed our lines.

3. (a) Work and new trenches.

A new trench appears to be in course of construction at F.6.a.8.2.

4. Trench Mortars.

A trench mortar fired on TOMBOIS FARM during the night.

5. See annexe overleaf.

Sd. W.P.Browne, Captain,
General Staff,
3rd. Cavalry Division.

1st. June, 1917.

Annexe to 3rd. Cavalry Division Summary 1st. June, 1917.

=*=*=*=*=*=*=*=*=*=*=*=*=*=*=*=*=*=*=*

1. <u>Information not included in yesterday's Summary.</u> (delayed).

   (i) 5.15 a.m. 31st. 5 men were seen working on a trench about X.30.d.5.6.
   (ii) An engine was seen in AUBENCHEUL, travelling N.W., early yesterday morning.

2. <u>From the Division on our Left.</u>

   (i) 2 small enemy parties were encountered by our patrols, on the night 30th/31st., in X.17.b. The enemy withdrew at once.
   (ii) 2 M.G's are reported to be firing from HONNECOURT WOOD - their suspected positions are X.11.b.4.3. and X.11.b.7.5.

3. <u>General.</u>

According to the German Official lists up to April 10th. the total number of prisoners in German Internment Camps are:-

	Officers.	Ranks.
French.	6,490	376,048.
Russian.	9,715	1,241,831.
Belgian.	657	41,795.
English.	1,471	38,192.
Serbians.	-	25,986.
Rumanians.	1,575	71,195.
Italians.	6	529.
Portugese.	-	14.
Japanese.	-	2.
Totals.	19,914.	1,795,574. other ranks.

Grand Total. 1,815,488.

=*=*=*=*=*=*=*=*=*=*=*=*=*=*=*=*=*=*=*

6

Appendix.10

3rd. Cavalry Division Intelligence Summary for 24 hours -

from 8 a.m. 1st. June to 8 a.m. 2nd. June, 1917.

1. Operations on Divisional Front.

(a) Our artillery.
8.55 a.m. our guns shelled earthwork at F.6.a.8.2., where Germans were seen working.
10.25. a.m. we shelled S.21.d.central, where 2 Germans were seen digging.
3.35 p.m. we retaliated on trench mortar, which was firing on the BIRDCAGE.

(b) Our snipers.
(i) A sniper from the BIRDCAGE shot a German 15^X in front of the German wire at X.30.c.4.3.
(ii) One of our snipers claims a hit on an enemy sniper at the N.W. corner of CANAL WOOD.

2. Hostile Attitude and Activity.

(a) Artillery.
(i) RONSSOY WOOD was again heavily "crumped" yesterday - 124 shells of heavy calibre (mostly 5.9's) falling there between 5.30 a.m. and 8.30 a.m.
(ii) PETIT PRIEL was again shelled intermittently.
(iii) At 11.45 a.m., X.22.c.central and X.21.d.5.3. were shelled.
(iv) EPEHY, TARGELLE RAVINE and K, L and M redoubts were all subjected to slight shelling during the day.
(v) At 5.30 a.m. today, a trench mortar bombarded the BIRDCAGE but was silenced by the fire of our guns.

(b) Movement.
(i) A battalion relief is thought to have taken place on the night 31st/1st. A wiring party who were 50^X - 100^X S. of the BIRDCAGE said that they heard considerable talking and movement in the enemy's trenches. Increased traffic, has also, been reported on the VILLERS OUTREAUX - BEAUREVOIR road during the last two days. This was especially noticeable yesterday.
(ii) 1.30 p.m., 26 mounted men followed by a 2 horsed wagon were seen going in a S. direction in T.21.d.
(iii) 1.30 p.m. men seen working at earthwork F.6.a.8.2.
(iv) 5.20 p.m 4 Germans walked from the road at S.2.d.5.1. in S.S.W. direction into the wood. This occurs daily and a path has been worn.
(v) A group of horses were seen (with horse-holders) about S.28.d.8.8.
(vi) Entrance to a dug-out was spotted on VENDHUILE - LA TERRIERE road at S.21.a.8.3. From this spot, 15 Germans were seen going singly to and from VENDHUILE and LA TERRIERE. One man was seen leading a black dog to VENDHUILE at 7.20 p.m. This is apparently a H.Qrs.

(c) Aviation.

An enemy aeroplane flew very low over our outpost line in our left sub-sector at 6.45 p.m. yesterday. No anti-aircraft gun engaged this machine, which had every opportunity of making a good reconnaissance.

3.   **First Army Front.**

    3 members of a British patrol, which went out on the night 24th/25th. May, S. of FRESNOY, lost their way and found themselves behind the line of German advanced posts.

    They remained out in concealment for 3 days, attempting each night to reach our lines. After having existed for 3 days without food or water, they succeeded in regaining our lines on the *fourth* night, bringing back important information.

2nd. June, 1917.
                                  Sd. W.P. Browne, Captain,
                                          General Staff,
                                      3rd. Cavalry Division.

3rd. Cavalry Division Intelligence Summary for 24 hours -

8 a.m. 2nd. to 8 a.m. 3rd. June, 1917.

1. Operations on Divisional Front.

   (a) Our Artillery.

   At 8.30 a.m., our "Hows". fired 5 rounds on to transport seen at A.4.a.3.4.
   At 8.32 a.m., our guns fired 2 rounds at a wagon on the LE CATELET - VENDHUILE road, causing the horse to bolt.
   At 10.15 a.m. and again at 1.30 p.m. we shelled the trench mortars in CANAL WOOD.
   Our guns, also, opened on a working party, seen in F.6.a.
   VENDHUILE and the enemy's trenches in X.30.a. and A.3.a. were also shelled during the day.

2. Hostile attitude and activity.

   (a) Artillery.

   (i) M.Post was shelled by 77 mm. guns from 7.45 a.m. to 8.40 a.m. and again from 1.45 p.m. to 2.20 p.m. apprently from the HONNECOURT direction.
   (ii) At 10.15 a.m. the enemy shelled X.23.a.7.9. for half an hour, also our outpost position just W. of CANAL WOOD.
   (iii) Our trenches in X.21.b. were shelled from 2.15 p.m. to 2.35 p.m. - 26 77 mm. shells being fired from the HONNECOURT direction

   (b) Movement.

   (i) Unusual movement was seen on the VENDHUILE - LE CATELET road during the morning.
   (ii) 11.35 a.m. 12 men were seen working on trench T.22.c.8.9.
   (iii) 2.30 p.m. party of 40 men walking in E. direction on GOUY - BEAUREVOIR road about BELLVUE FARM.
   (iv) 6.20 p.m. party of 20 men working on trenches at Farm, T.20.b.9.9.
   (v) 8.30 p.m. 6 Germans working in Sand Pit, S.10.c.4.9. - appeared to be working a pump.
   (vi) 4 single motor lorries, seen at different times during the day, on the VILLERS OUTREAUX - BEAUREVOIR road - 3 were going S. and one N.

   (c) Aviation.

   Hostile air activity was normal.

3. Hostile Defences.
   (a) New work etc.
   Six black mounds were seen in sunken road in S.20.b., which Artillery Observing Officer reports as a possible battery position.
   (b) Demolitions.
   A cloud of smoke was seen rising from buildings about "LES TRANCHEES" (X.12.c.) This lasted for about 15 minutes.

                                        Sd. W.P.Browne, Captain,
                                           General Staff,
3rd. June, 1917.   3rd. Cavalry Division.

Annexe to 3rd. Cavalry Division Summary 3rd. June, 1917.

Neighbouring Divisions.

1. A belt of wire (4 stakes wide) is reported from CANAL WOOD about X.23.b.6.9. to X.23.b.6.0.
   X.14.a.6.9.

2. The short length of trench in S.20.a. contained about 30 men on 31st. evening, and previous evening about 18 men were seen there.

3. Men have been seen to leave a point S.20.a.1.1. at dawn, others have been noticed in the QUARRY about S.20.d.2.9.

French Wireless.

Aviation.

During period 7th. to 31st. May, 32 German aeroplanes have been completely destroyed on French Front, in addition 57 other machines were seriously damaged. Capt. GUYNEMER brought down five aeroplanes (4 on the same day), two of which were brought down at an interval of one minute. The total number of hostile aeroplanes destroyed by GUYNEMER is 43.

German Money.

German money has now reached a further low record. 100 marks being quoted at 73 francs, thus 100 francs in Germany would only be worth 58.50 francs in France.

3rd Cavalry Division Intelligence Summary period

8 a.m. 3rd to 8 a.m. 4th June, 1917.

1. OPERATIONS ON DIVISIONAL FRONT.
   Our Artillery.
   We shelled the following localities during the day :-
      LA TERRIERE, VENDHUILLE, OSSUS WOOD,
      and the Quarries at S.14.d.1.2.

2. HOSTILE ATTITUDE AND ACTIVITY.

   (a) Artillery.
       Between 9 a.m. and 2-30 p.m. the enemy put over 100 8" shells into EPEHY - from the direction of LE CATELET.
       From 6-0 p.m. to 7-0 p.m. the Quarry in X.17.c. was shelled with 4·2's. The true bearing taken from the S.E. corner of the Quarry was approx. 50°.
       RONSSOY village and wood were heavily shelled during the morning with 4·2's and 5·9's.

   (b) Movement.
       (i) 4 Germans were seen coming out of the wood at S.16.a.9.1. They walked towards the Quarry and appeared to be patrolling telephone wires.
       (ii) At X.23.d.4.0., two Germans were seen to crawl for a few yards and disappear into a shell hole, where they continued working throughout the day. It was thought that they were making a M.G. emplacement.
       (iii) 12-30 p.m. Small party were seen working on trench about T.20.b.6.9.
       (iv) 6-10 p.m. A party of 17 men were seen moving W. from BELLEVUE FARM - with intervals between sections.
       (v) 6-40 p.m. Party of 6 men were seen at the same Farm, also moving W. Considerable movement was observed here during the day.
       (vi) 8-10 p.m. A party of 9 Germans seen working about M.36.c.3.8.

   (c) Aviation.
       9-15 a.m. 6 hostile planes manoeuvred over our lines, but disappeared in a Northerly direction on being fired at.
       At 3-55 p.m. and again at 8-30 p.m., 4 hostile machines came over, but withdrew immediately on being engaged by our A.A. guns.

3. NEIGHBOURING DIVISION. - REPORT FROM.

   RANCOURT FARM and BONABUS FARM.
   A brushwood screen has been commenced on the Northern side of the road, from the road junction in S.11.a. to BONABUS FARM.
   A portion of RANCOURT FARM has been demolished and the bricks carried to the trench and dumped at S.10.a.8.8. BONABUS and RANCOURT Farms are suspected to be H.Q's owing to the movement of cyclists, signallers and transport to and from these places.
   The Road at S.16.a.1.9. shews signs of considerable use by heavy transport during the night 2nd/3rd.

(sd) W.P. BROWNE, Captain,
4th June, 1917.   G.S., 3rd Cavalry Division.

3rd. Cavalry Division Intelligence Summary for 24 hours -

from 8 a.m. 4th. to 8 a.m. 5th. June, 1917.

1. Operations on Divisional Front.

    (a) Our Artillery.

    We shelled the following localities during the day - VENDHUILE - LA TERRIERE - Sunk road in X.30.a.6.1. - CANAL WOOD - and the QUARRY in S.14.d.

    (b) Our Machine Guns.

    1,000 rounds were fired into OSSUS village during the early part of the night.

2. Hostile Attitude and Activity.

    (a) Artillery.

    8 a.m. 'G'Post and PETIT PRIEL FARM were shelled - 18 4.2's being fired.
    During the morning, 4 5.9's were fired into ST.EMILIE and 4 4.2's into MALASSISE FARM.
    Between 11.30 a.m. and 12.30 p.m. the enemy fired 20 77 mm. shells into X.17.c.
    The railway line in W.23.central was shelled with 11 4.2's during the afternoon.

    (b) Movement.

    (i) At 9 a.m. and again at 10 a.m. and 6.10 p.m., clouds of smoke were seen to rise from RANCOURT FARM.
    (ii) At 10.35 a.m. 3 transport wagons were seen moving E. past BELLEVUE FARM.
    (iii) 5 p.m. 2 men seen entering communication trench in sandbank, S.10.c.4.9.
    (iv) 8.40 p.m. 2 men seen to walk from HONNECOURT and enter a pit about S.14.a.8.6., carrying what appeared to be boxes of M.G. ammunition.
    (v) A working party was observed at a small trench in X.24.d.0.4. Heavy planks and girders were taken into the trench during the afternoon.
    (vi) Considerable movement was seen between BANTOUZELLE & VAUCELLES WOOD - men walking about in ones and twos, carrying small boxes or shells.
    (vii) Small parties were seen W of AUBENCHEUL and in S.23 and S.15.
    (viii) Movement was seen on the RANCOURT FARM - BANTOUZELLE and VILLERS OUTREAUX - BEAUREVOIR roads. Considerable movement of vehicles and of small parties of men is reported to have been observed at BELLEVUE FARM.

    (c) Aviation.

    An enemy observation balloon is reported to have ascended at 10.5 a.m. from behind LA TERRIERE WOOD.
    Hostile aeroplanes were seen at 9a.m. 9.35 a.m. 9.40 a.m. 3.15 p.m. 8 p.m. and 8.35 p.m.
    At 9.35 a.m. one enemy machine flew up and down our line several times before making off East.

3. Hostile Defences.

    (a) Work and new trenches.

    (i) Fresh work was seen at a trench in X.30.c.5.0.
    (ii) Fresh earth was seen to have been thrown up about T.20.b.6.4
    (iii) Sounds of talking and digging was heard to come from the neighbourhood of the small trench in X.24.c.2.5. between 11 p.m. & 2 a.m.

4. **Miscellaneous - Rockets.**

"Golden Rain" and Green and Red Rockets have been seen the last two nights, for the most part just N. of our sector.

It is now thought that the greater number of these were sent up by the enemy.

They went up from various points, and when, as often happened, a rocket went up near a searchlight, the 2 appeared to be worked in conjunction - the searchlight was immediately turned on and shrapnel was seen to burst very high in the air.

The searchlights were due N.E. from M.Post (i.e. E. of BANTOUZELLE).

5. **Neighbouring Division.**

The Division on our left reports as follows:-

(i) An O.P. is suspected at the trench S.3.d.3.4. as 2 men left HINDENBURG LINE S.10.a.5.4. and went into the trench, stopping at intervals, as if to examine telephone wire.

(ii) **Work and Defences.**
The enemy is reported to be working on the Northern side of HONNECOURT WOOD. Working party was observed on the road between S.10.c.7.5. and S.10.b.3.4.

(iii) **Machine Guns.**
Hostile M.Gs are reported firing during the night from X.24.a.4.4. and X.11.d.4.7., also from the N.W. and S.W. corners of HONNECOURT WOOD.

5th. June, 1917.

Sd. W.P.Browne, Captain,
General Staff,
3rd. Cavalry Division.

3rd Cavalry Division Intelligence Summary, period
8 a.m. 5th to 8 a.m. 6th June, 1917.

1. **OPERATIONS.**

   (a) <u>Patrols.</u>
   (i) A patrol went out last night to reconnoitre the suspected M.G. Emplacement at X.23.d.4.0. (see 3rd Cav. Div. Summary 4th June, para. 2 (b) (ii).). The patrol got to within 20^x of this post; they found it occupied and heard voices. They could see no signs of wire. They waited there for over one hour, but the enemy did not fire, and the patrol is unable to confirm the presence of a M.G. there.
   There is a small post 100^x N. of this, which was also reconnoitred. This was untenanted, and appeared quite disused.
   (ii) A patrol went out last night to reconnoitre the dummy guns at X.23.b. Central. They found this place strongly wired and there appeared to be a trench 40^x behind this wire. Voices were heard and Very Lights went up from this trench. The patrol stayed out by the wire for an hour, but nothing further could be seen.

   (b) <u>Our Artillery.</u>
   (i) 9-40 a.m. Our 13 pdrs put 4 rounds into the QUARRY at S.14.c., where movement was seen.
   (ii) 12-15 p.m. We fired 56 H.E. shells into S.14.a.2½.7. where a telephone exchange is suspected.
   (iii) We also shelled the following localities during the afternoon :- S.15.a.7.8.; S.Roads . . X.14.a.7.7.; X.23.d.7.0.; Road at A.1.a.2.5.; OSSUS WOOD ; LA TERRIERE; N. side of CANAL WOOD.

2. **HOSTILE ATTITUDE AND ACTIVITY.**

   (a) <u>Artillery.</u>
   (i) LITTLE PRIEL FARM was shelled intermittently during the day.
   (ii) At 9-0 a.m. 100 4·2's and 5·9's were fired into LEMPIRE and RONSSOY.
   (iii) From 10-0 a.m. to 11-30 a.m. the enemy shelled the ridge from X.17.a.6.2. to X.11.c.5.2. with 4·2's - from the direction of HONNECOURT.
   (iv) CATELET COPSE and the BIRDCAGE were slightly shelled in the morning, and the BIRDCAGE QUARRY was shelled at intervals during the night, especially between 11-45 p.m. and 1-0 a.m.
   (v) 7-30 a.m. An enemy 77 mm gun put 5 shells into L Redoubt, 2 of which burst on concussion, and one by time fuze, the other 2 being "duds".

   (c) <u>Aviation.</u>
   Hostile aeroplanes came over at 8-15 p.m., but disappeared immediately.
   At 6-0 a.m., an enemy machine flew over our trenches for a considerable time and then disappeared.

3. **HOSTILE DEFENCES.**
   At 10-0 p.m. a working party of 8 men came along the N. side of OSSUS WOOD from about X.24.c.3.1. to X.29.b.7.7. where they commenced wiring and fortifying a post of some sort. One shot was fired by a sniper and the party bolted and did not return.

   6th June, 1917.
   (sd) W.P. BROWNE, Captain,
   G.S., 3rd Cavalry Division.

3rd. Cavalry Division Intelligence Summary for 24 hours

from 8 a.m. 6th. to 8 a.m. 7th. June, 1917.

1. **Operations on Divisional Front.**

   (a) <u>Our patrols.</u>

   A patrol which went out at midnight from X.23.c., heard the enemy working in OSSUS WOOD.

   (b) <u>Our Artillery.</u>
   At midnight, our artillery assisted the Division on our right to put up a barrage in front of their left, sub-sector, in response to a S.O.S. signal.
   It has since transpired that this S.O.S. Signal was put up by the enemy.

2. **Hostile Attitude & Activity.**

   (a) <u>Artillery.</u>
   (i) X.14.a. and d. were shelled by 15 cm's. and 4.2's in the morning.
   (ii) At 10.15 a.m. 4 4.2's were fired into 'G' post from the direction of LA TERRIERE.
   (iii) At about 8 p.m. 20 77mm. shells fell in L.Post, causing one casualty. This gun seemed to be firing from the W. edge of LA TERRIERE.
   (iv) At 3.5 a.m. 20 H.E. shells were fired into X.28.b. and d.
   (v) At 6.50 a.m. the enemy put 20 H.E. shells just to the left of our Outpost line. These appeared to be fired from the same gun as in (iii) above.

   (b) <u>Movement.</u>
   Abnormal movement (largely in a W. direction) was seen on the following roads.
   P. BEAUREVOIR - GOUY.
   Q. AUBENCHEUL-aux-BOIS - VENDHUILE.
   R. LA TERRIERE - VENDHUILE.

   (i) 9.30 a.m. 2 G.S. wagons seen on P.road going E. past BELLEVUE FARM.
   (ii) 10.30 a.m. 10 men seen going W. at same place.
   (iii) 10.45 a.m. 6 parties(moving at 50^x interval), of about 20 men each, were seen going W. at same place.
   (iv) 1.45 p.m. 21 Germans seen going W. in pairs at about 200^x interval, on R. road, S.21.c.central. They were later seen returning.
   (v) 1 p.m. to 2 p.m. A large party of 50 - 100 Germans were seen moving S.W. on Q. road, at S.23.c. and S.22 d. They moved in half-sections at about 100^x interval.
   2 p.m. our artillery fired one round at this road about S.28.b.0.3. The men who were crossing the high ground from S.23.c., were seen to stop, but they soon moved on.

   (c) <u>Aviation.</u>

   (i) At 1 p.m. 3 enemy machines were seen at a high altitude. At 8.55 p.m. one H.A. flew along over our line and disappeared South.
   (ii) At 1.5 p.m., one of our aeroplanes was brought down in flames about A.8.central, by enemy's A.A. guns.

3. Hostile Defences.

(a) Work and Wire.

Men have been seen working in a shell hole about X.23.d.2.4. This place can be seen from the BIRDCAGE.

General News.

The Second Army attacked this morning and had captured WYTSCHAETE and MESSINES and about 2,000 prisoners by 11 a.m.

Late News.

The Westerly movement reported above is continuing today, to an even greater extent.

7th. June, 1917.

Sd. W.P.Browne, Capt,
General Staff,
3rd. Cavalry Division.

Addendum to 3rd. Cavalry Division Summary for 24
hours from 8. a.m. 6th to 8 a.m. 7th. June 1917.

2 <u>Hostile Attitude and Activity.</u>

   (b) <u>Enemy Movement.</u>

     (vi) 8pm 2 platoons seen marching from PIENNE (S.23.a.7.0) due W. towards the HINDENBURG LINE.
     They were followed soon after by a large party (estimated by observer at 100 men), who proceeded in the same direction.

     (vii) 8.15 to 8.30 p.m. A transport column of 15 or more wagons (or lorries - the light was failing) was seen moving slowly S.W. along LA TERRIERE - VENDHUILE road, in S.15.d.

     (viii) The usual movement of very small parties and single men was also seen.

     (ix) 11.45 p.m. - 1 a.m. transport was heard - thought to be about DE LA L'EAU.

     (x) Lateral Movement: LE CATELET - VENDHUILE road.
     11 a.m. Several Germans seen on this road.
     12 noon to 1 p.m. between 30 and 40 men passed along this road - the largest party was 14.

7th. June, 1917.

                              Captain,
                    G.S., 3rd. Cavalry Division.

3rd. Cavalry Division Intelligence Summary for 24 hours
from 8 a.m. 7th. to 8 a.m. 8th. June, 1917.

1. Operations on Divisional Front.

   (a) Our patrols.

   (i) A patrol of an officer and 3 men went out at 12 midnight from No. 1 post, to reconnoitre the salient in the enemy's line at X.23.d.8½.4½., where 2 M.G's are suspected - vide CATELET Sheet 1/20,000.
   They got close up to the salient and could see a post or emplacement of some kind on the road. The enemy could be heard talking and the post appeared strongly held.
   The wire did not look very formidable, but the grass in front had been cut. The wire is continuous to the N.N.E. and to the S.S.E., but no sign of a continuous trench could be seen and this appears to be an isolated post. The patrol were fired upon from the S. and withdrew.

   (ii) An N.C.O's patrol went out to continue the reconnaissance of the area in X.23.b.central, where the dummy guns are (ref. 3rd. Cav. Div. Summary 6th. June, para 1 (a) ii). The wire referred to in the previous report was found to be E. of the dummy guns (of which there are 3), and identical with that shown in X.24.a. on the CATALET Sheet. They heard sounds of hammering in the E. end of CANAL WOOD. They were not fired at.

   (b) Our Artillery.

   (i) 5.15 p.m., 10 rounds 13 pr. H.E. were fired at enemy movement, seen between F.6.a. and the KNOLL.
   (ii) 6 p.m. some enemy were observed at A.4.a.3.4. They were engaged by a Howitzer Battery.
   (iii) 7.5 p.m. our guns shelled RANCOURT FARM and set it on fire. One big building has been gutted out.
   (iv) We shelled the following localities during the day; OSSUS Village - Sunk road (X.30.a.), OSSUS WOOD - S.20.b - W. end of VENDHUILE-F.6.a. & c.

   (c) Our snipers.

   5.15 p.m. - A German came out from N. side of OSSUS WOOD to a trench in X.24.c. One of our snipers fired. The German staggered and fell. He was not seen to move again. This is corroborated by snipers from one of the other posts.

2. Hostile Attitude & Activity.

   (a) Artillery.

   Hostile shelling was decidedly below normal yesterday. 45 shells from a 5.9 were fired into ST.EMILIE and the valley between that place and VILLERS FAUCON - at intervals between 8.30 a.m. and 3 p.m. . The first 4 rounds were fired at regular intervals of 15 minutes.

   (b) Movement.

   (i) 8.55 a.m. 2 large lorries moving W. past BELLVUE FARM.

(ii)

(ii)   9.5 a.m.   11 men seen walking along road from RANCOURT FARM to BANTOUZELLE, in two's and three's at 100^X intervals.
(iii) 10.30 a.m. 5 men seen working on wire and trenches in S.21.central.
(iv)   10.45 a.m. Same 5 men appeared to enter a dug-out; a few minutes later, smoke issued from this black patch, which seems to be a dug-out entrance.
(v)   11.25 a.m. Smoke was seen issuing from the place described in (iv) above. Soon after, gusts of flame were clearly seen to come from the same place, giving the appearance of a burning dug-out.
(vi)   11.55 a.m. - 12.30p.m. About 300 men are estimated to have passed BELLEVUE FARM, moving in a W. direction. They were at first marching in sections at 50^X distance. They subsequently opened out and moved along both sides of the road. 2 motor cars and 2 lorries were seen to go E. down the centre of the road.
(vii) 1.35 p.m. 70 men passed BELLEVUE FARM, marching towards GOUY, with similar intervals and on either side of the road.
(viii) 3.10 p.m. 4 parties of 8 men each, with 50^X between parties, passed BELLEVUE Farm, going in an E. direction.
(ix)   6 - 6.40 p.m. About 20 men moved S.W. in ½ sections along the PIENNE - VENDHUILE road.
(x)   7.50p.m - 8.20 p.m. Flashes were seen about S.21.central, which seemed to be undoubtedly lamp-signalling in Morse Code.
(xi)   7.55 p.m. A large party of men could be seen at PIENNE. They marched off almost immediately along the road to VENDHUILE. The light was failing and numbers could not be estimated.
(xii) (Reported by Artillery O.O. - vide para 1 (b) (i) above).

      5.20 p.m. Parties of Germans were seen in the trench between the "KNOLL" and F.6.a., several groups were also seen in shell holes in front of the trench, baling out water. These appeared to be Machine Gun emplacements, well hidden by the long grass.

Summary.

The abnormal Westerly movement was continued yesterday - only one party being seen to go East.

(c) Aviation.

11. 45 a.m. 4 enemy machines were seen at a high altitude.

Between 7 p.m. and 8.30 p.m. 3 single machines were seen No hostile balloons were reported opposite our sector.

3.   Hostile Defences.

(a) Work.

(i) A new bank of earth was observed at about S.21.a.0.3.
(ii) New work is reported in the SANDPIT or QUARRY, S.10.c.3.9.

(b) Wire.

Attention is drawn to Patrol Reports in para 1 (a).
The following particulars were obtained by the N.C.O's patrol, with

regard

8

3rd CAVALRY DIVISION INTELLIGENCE SUMMARY for 24 hours
8 a.m. 8th to 8 a.m. 9th June, 1917.

1. **OPERATIONS ON DIVISIONAL FRONT.**

   (a) **Patrols.**
   (i) At 12-30 a.m. last night, a patrol of 2 Officers and 3 men went out to reconnoitre the M.G. emplacement at X.23.d.8½.4½. They got up to the wire and report that the emplacement appeared to be unoccupied and to have received a direct hit from one of our guns during the afternoon.
   Observers had been posted to watch the flash of any M.G., which might fire, but no enemy M.G. opened fire from anywhere near that position. It is, therefore, thought that this is definitely the emplacement, from which the enemy has been in the habit of firing towards PETIT PRIEL FARM and CATELET COPSE.
   (ii) A patrol of 1 N.C.O. and 3 men went out last night and proceeded South of the dummy guns, to reconnoitre the enemy's wire about X.24.a.1.1. and found the wire continuous from about that point to CANAL Wood.
   The enemy was again heard working in CANAL Wood.

   (b) **Our Artillery.**
   We fired on the following localities during the day:-
   VENDHUILE, OSSUS WOOD, X.23.d., RANCOURT FARM, FRANQUE Wood.

   (c) **Our Snipers.**
   About 4-30 p.m. 2 shots were fired at a German who was observing through a telescope of some sort from behind a bush. The man was seen to crawl painfully away. Observers in another post, also, reported this to have been a hit.

2. **HOSTILE ATTITUDE AND ACTIVITY.**
   (a) (i) **Artillery.**
   9-0 a.m. - 11-0 a.m. the enemy shelled W.30.a. and b. (W. of PEZIERE) with 50 shells from a 4.1 H.V. Gun - true bearing 102° (3rd Cav.Div.Artillery Summary.)
   9-30 a.m. a 10 c.m. gun put 40 shells into EPEHY, from the direction of VENDHUILE.
   10 a.m. - 3-0 p.m. VILLERS FAUCON and E.23.d. shelled with 52 8" shells from the Le CATELET direction.
   There was again an almost entire absence of shelling in the forward area.

   (ii) **Trench Mortars.**
   The Quarries at X.17.c.3.3. were trench-mortared by the enemy at 2-0 a.m.

   (b) **Movement.**
   (i) 8-35 a.m. 16 men seen going in a S.W. direction on the LA PANNERIE - VENDHUILE Road.
   (ii) 10-0 a.m. - 10-40 a.m. Activity of wheeled traffic in an E. direction past BELLEVUE FARM - 12 vehicles.
   (iii) 9-15 a.m. 22 men seen at fallen tree (M.33.d.3.6.). They were in ½ sections; 7 men were carrying long poles.
   (iv) 1-45 p.m. movement of wheeled traffic in an E. direction past BELLEVUE FARM - 5 vehicles, 4 men walking behind each.
   (v) 2-5 p.m. 68 men marched by sections (with intervals) in a W. direction past BELLEVUE FARM.
   (vi) at 7-35 p.m. what appears to be lamp-signalling, was again seen ∧ S.21 Central. But this was NOT in Morse Code.
   (vii) The usual movement of small parties and individuals was observed in the HINDENBURG Line, W. of LA TERRIERE.

   (c)/

- 2 -

  (c) Aviation.
    10-30 a.m. one of our bombing Squadrons crossed the German lines, but met a Squadron of about 15 enemy machines (Albatross and Aviatik) and was forced to return - all our machines got back safely.
    3 other enemy machines were seen in the course of the 24 hours.

3. HOSTILE DEFENCES.

  (a) Work and new trenches.
    (1) A new post (an improved shell hole?) is reported at X.23.d.7.2., which was used by the German, whom our sniper hit, as reported para 1 (c) overleaf.

  (b) Wire.
    From the report received from the N.C.O. i/c of the patrol described in para. 1 (a) (ii) overleaf, it appears that there is a continuous single apron of wire from OSSUS WOOD to CANAL WOOD, as shown on the CATELET Sheet - a report on this wire was given in para. 3 (b) of yesterday's Summary.
    Our patrols have been up to this wire at several points during the past week, and on no occasion has the enemy been met with, in front of his own wire.

4. HOSTILE ORGANIZATION.
  (a) Dumps.
    A Dump is suspected at M.36.c.3.8., where men have been seen working - apparently handling or carrying boxes, etc.
  (b) Railways.
    An enemy party was observed working just S. of BASKET WOOD, on what appears to be a light railway

5. BATTERY POSITIONS.
    (1) L Post was shelled on the 7th instant by a gun, which was located on the forward slope, just E. of FRANQUE WOOD at S.8.d.8.5. - true bearing from L Post was 63°.
    (ii) 2 - 5.9 Hows. were seen firing in VENDHUILE this morning - they are not yet located accurately.

6. NEIGHBOURING DIVISIONS.
    (1) The enemy is occupying the crater at X.17.b.2.7.; it is probable that this post contains 3 machine guns.*

    (ii) Machine Guns. A M.G. is suspected at X.23.b.5.9.

                                    (Sd) W.P. BROWNE, Captain,
9th June, 1917.   G.S., 3rd Cavalry Division.

* This is undoubtedly the crater shewn at
  X.17.b.4.9. on the CATELET Sheet.

regard to the wire in S.24.a.

One apron - 3 rows of posts - centre posts 4' high - outside posts 1' - width of entanglement 10' - there is loose wire mixed up in it.

(c) Machine Guns.

Following report from Right Sub-sector:-
"2 enemy machine guns very active during the night and 1 continued firing during the day. They appeared to be firing from the enemy's outpost line in X.23.d. and X.24.c.

One gun, whose flashes were plainly visible, is reported firing from about 10^x S. of the road (i.e. about X.23.d.9.3., i.e. a little further South than where it was previously located).

The other gun was thought to be in the same trench but close to the edge of the wood. This gun fired intermittently up the valley, into the bank directly behind CATALET COPSE.

4. Miscellaneous.

(a) Gas Alarm.

At 2.40 a.m. a "Golden Rain" rocket was sent up and seen by a sentry in our Right Sub-sector, who sounded a Strombos Horn. The alarm was not taken up, as it was thought that the rocket had been put up by the enemy - there being no sign of any gas.

(b) Delayed Report.

On the night June 5th/6th., our M.G's fired 500 rounds into OSSUS Village. Listening posts report considerable shouting and confusion, apparently as a result of this.

5. Neighbouring Divisions.

(1) In the Right Sector strong patrols attempted to cut out the enemy at the points at which he had been identified the previous night, namely, the crater at X.17.b.4.8. and the post about X.5.d.5.8. In both cases, however, the positions were found unoccupied. The patrol which attacked the crater went on until heavily fired at from the outskirts of HONNECOURT Village.

(2) Hostile guns were observed as follows:-
(i) Firing from S.9.a.25.55 - 6 rounds at 8 p.m., located by smoke puffs. Visible from X.5.c.7.3.
(ii) Guns firing from about S.9.central - located by flash and smoke.

Sd. W.P.Browne, Captain,
General Staff,
3rd. Cavalry Division.

8th. June, 1917.

N O T I C E.
==*=*=*

MAP REFERENCES.

IN ALL 3RD. CAVALRY DIVISION SUMMARIES FROM TODAY'S DATE, THE LE CATALET 1/20,000 SHEET WILL BE USED FOR ALL REFERENCES TO THE AREA WHICH IT COVERS, AS IT IS MORE UP-TO-DATE THAN THE REGULAR SERIES.

==*=*=*=*=*=*=*=*=*=*=*=*=*=*=*=*=*=*

3rd. Cavalry Division Intelligence Summary for 24 hours -
from 8 a.m. 9th. to 8 a.m. 10th. June, 1917.

1. **Operations on Divisional Front.**

    (a) *Patrols.*

    (i) An officer's patrol report having heard an enemy working party in CANAL WOOD last night. The patrol which went out a quarter of a mile in front of our advanced post encountered no wire.

    (ii) At 11 p.m. a patrol visited the 12 Willow trees in TOMBOIS VALLEY at F.5.d.1.3., and remained there until 2 a.m., but nothing was observed. A working had been observed in F.5.d.0.1. at 7.30 p.m.

    (b) *Our Artillery.*

    We fired on the following localities during the day - PUTNEY VALLEY, the crossing of road and trench at X.23.d.8½.4½, and the QUARRIES at S.30.d.7.7. and S.14.a.3.7.

2. **Hostile Attitude and Activity.**

    (a) *Artillery.*

    8.15 a.m. LITTLE PRIEL FARM was shelled from the direction of VENDHUILE with 77 mm. shells.
    At 8.30 a.m. and again between 12 and 1 p.m. the QUARRY at X.29.d.2.3. was shelled with 4.2 cm. shells from the direction of VENDHUILE.
    1.15 p.m. to 4.45 p.m. LITTLE PRIEL FARM shelled with 10 rounds of 4.2 cm.
    2.30 p.m. to 2.55 p.m. "M" Post shelled with 15 rounds of 77 mm.
    2.30 p.m. 3 10 cm. shells were fired on BIRDCAGE Trench.

    (b) *Movement.*

    (i) At 7.10 p.m. 2 men were observed to walk across country from S.14.a. to the trenches at S.10.c.4.6.
    (ii) Between 3.15 and 4 p.m. a number of lorries were seen on the LE CATELET main road S.E. of BASKET WOOD.
    (iii) At 7.15 p.m. 6 lorries and 2 limbers were seen moving East past BELLEVUE FARM on the GOUY - BEAUREVOIR road.
    (iv) During the day small parties of men were observed in the direction of LA TERRIERE.
    (v) A small fire was seen in the afternoon at S.21.d.2.8.
    (vi) Fresh earth has been thrown up in S.21.central.

    (c) *Machine Guns.*

    CATELET VALLEY was swept at intervals by M.G. fire during the day.

    (d) *Aviation.*

    At 2.30 p.m and again at 8.25 p.m. H.A. appeared over our lines

3. **Neighbouring Divisions.**

    (i) A party of about 40 Germans were seen at 6.10 p.m. apparently digging in front of RANCOURT FARM from S.10.a.8.7. to S.4.c.6.2.
    (ii) The road between HONNECOURT and TERRIERE WOOD shews new transport tracks at S.10.c.6.3.

Sd. W.R.Brandt, Lieut, for Capt.
10th. June, 1917.   General Staff, 3rd. Cavalry Division.

3rd Cavalry Division Intelligence Summary for 24 hours from 8 a.m. 10th to 8 a.m. 11th June, 1917.

1. **Operations on Divisional Front.**

    (a) **Our patrols.**

    A patrol went along the N. edge of CANAL WOOD last night. They could not form an estimate as to how far they went, as it was a very dark night. The distance is estimated at 200x. No enemy post or wire was seen outside the wood. Enemy were again heard working inside the Wood.

    (b) **Our artillery.**

    (i) A working party was seen at X.24.c.1.8. and was effectively engaged by our 13 prs.
    (ii) The following localities were shelled by us during the day: OSSUS WOOD, The KNOLL, and enemy's trenches in A.1.a.
    (iii) There was considerable artillery activity during the night. In retaliation for the enemy's bombardment of the sector on our right of our own right flank, we shelled the enemy heavily between 10 and 11 p.m. and again between 12.30 a.m. and 1 a.m.

2. **Hostile Attitude and Activity.**

    (a) **Artillery.**

    (i) 12 noon - 12.30 p.m. Enemy's guns from the direction of LA TERRIERE, put 20   77mm. shells into LITTLE PRIEL FARM and 10 more at 3.40 p.m.
    (ii) 3.45 p.m. - 13 77mm. shells were fired at "G" Post from the same direction.
    (iii) 3.50 p.m. - 5 77mm. shells were fired into 13 COPSE from same direction. All 5 were "duds".

    (b) **Movement.**
    Visibility was very bad all day.
    (i) The usual movement of small parties and individuals was seen in Squares S.14, 15, 20 and 21.
    (ii) A working party of about 15 men were seen in X.24.c.1.8. and dispersed by our artillery.

    (c) **Aviation.**
    At 7.45 p.m. an enemy machine flew very low over our line but was not engaged by our A.A. guns.
    At 8.25 p.m. an enemy machine was over our line for 20 minutes.

3. **Hostile Defences.**

    (a) **Work and New trenches.**

    (i) Further signs of new work . are reported in S.21.central.

    S. of OSSUS WOOD.

    (ii) The line through F.6.a. is now prolonged N. of the LITTLE PRIEL - VENDHUILE road to about X.30.c.6.4., when it is lost to sight over the sky line - it is probably being prolonged to join the VENDHUILE - OSSUS WOOD Line (which runs from A.1.a. through X.30. central).
    There is a single row of wire in front of this trench. No work can be seen other than the actual front line.
    (iii) Air photos, taken on 6th. inst., show the following additions to the VENDHUILE - OSSUS WOOD Line.
    From X.30.a.4.6., the enemy has made a sap running out W.S.W. for about 100x.

    From

From X.30.a.4.7. he has connected up a line of shell holes, which now forms a traversed fire trench running to the S. edge of the wood in X.30.a.2.8.

N. of OSSUS WOOD.

(iv) Air photos taken on 6th. inst. show that the enemy has deepened and improved his fire-trench from the N. edge of OSSUS WOOD to X.23.d.8½.4½. (OSSUS WOOD - CANAL WOOD Line).

The remainder of this line (i.e. the short lengths of trench in X.24.a. and c.) does not appear to have undergone any alteration and conforms to the LE CATALET Sheet.

OSSUS WOOD.

(v) As regards OSSUS WOOD itself, it would appear certain that the VENDHUILE - OSSUS WOOD and the OSSUS WOOD - CANAL WOOD Lines are connected up by a trench running from X.30.a.2.8. to X.24.a.0.0., which has a barricade of felled trees and French wire in front of it (vide 3rd. Cav. Div. Summary 29th. May para 1 (a) " Reconnaissance of OSSUS WOOD".)

Sd. W.P.Browne, Capt,
General Staff,
3rd. Cavalry Division.

11th. June, 1917.

3rd CAVALRY DIVISION INTELLIGENCE SUMMARY
period from 8 a.m. 11th to 8 a.m. 12th June, 1917.

1. **OPERATIONS ON DIVISIONAL FRONT.**

    (a) <u>Our Patrols.</u>
    An Officers' patrol which went out in the neighbourhood of 12 WILLOWS heard a wiring party at work in the direction of the KNOLL; otherwise all was quiet.

    (b) <u>Our Artillery.</u>
    During the day, the enemy's trenches at F.6.a. and his posts in the neighbourhood of OSSUS WOOD were shelled.

2. **HOSTILE ATTITUDE AND ACTIVITY.**

    (a) <u>Artillery.</u>
    (i) During the day, PIGEON RAVINE, CATELET COPSE, LITTLE PRIEL FARM and TOMBOIS FARM were shelled at intervals from the direction of LA TERRIERE.
    (ii) At 2-30 p.m. "G" Post was shelled with 9 77 mm shells from the direction of MACQUINCOURT FARM.
    (iii) At 3-5 p.m. X.23.c. and at 5-30 p.m. X.22.c. were shelled by 4.2's. F.O.O. report this gun to be close up, but has not yet located its exact position.
    (iv) Between 7 and 8 a.m. this morning, No. 13 COPSE was shelled with H.E.

    (b) <u>Movement.</u>
    Visibility was very bad all day.
    (i) At 10 a.m., and again in the afternoon, men were seen to be occupying the trench at X.30.c.6.0.
    (ii) During the afternoon, small parties of men were observed moving about in S.26.b.
    (iii) At 2-15 p.m., a fire was seen at S.21. Central.

    (c) <u>Aviation.</u>
    At 4-55 p.m., two H.A. crossed our lines, but returned on encountering one of our machines. Between 5 a.m. and 7 a.m. one H.A. manoeuvred along our lines for two hours. It was prevented from crossing our lines by our A.A. Guns.

3. **HOSTILE DEFENCES.**

    (i) <u>Wire.</u>
    Several coils of wire were seen behind the enemy's trench at X.32.c.6.0.

    (ii) <u>Machine Guns.</u>
    A machine gun is suspected at X.29.b.1.9.

12th June, 1917.
(Sd) W.R. BRANDT, Lieut.,
for G.S., 3rd Cavalry Division.

CORRIGENDUM.

Reference yesterday's Summary, para., 3 (v), line 3.
For X.24.a.0.0. please read X.24.c.0.0.

3rd. Cavalry Division Intelligence Summary for 24 hours –

From 8 a.m. 12th. to 8 a.m. 13th. June, 1917.

1. **Operations on Divisional Front.**

   (a) *Our patrols.*

   (i) About 11 p.m. an Officer's patrol went out to the 12 WILLOWS. They report hearing wagons on the LEMPIRE – VENDHUILE road. They encountered no enemy.

   (ii) At 12 midnight, an officer's patrol went out from No. 1 post, to reconnoitre towards the enemy's front line in X.24.a.
   They reached a point about X.24.a.0.2. From here they detected a listening post about 20^x in front of the enemy's wire.
   They heard a small wiring party at work, about X.24.a.1.0.
   They heard movement in CANAL WOOD, about X.23.b.9.9.
   They remained out in close proximity to the enemy's wire until 1.40 a.m., without being disturbed by the enemy.

   (b) *Our Artillery.*

   9 a.m.   Our 4.5 Hows. fired 31 rounds into VENDHUILE.
   12 noon)
      to   )   Our 18 prs. shelled the enemy's front line
   4.30 p.m.)   from X.24.a.2.3. to X.24.c.C.8.

2. **Hostile Attitude and Activity.**

   (a) *Artillery.*

   6.30 a.m.)
      to   ) 12th. 50 8" shells were fired into F.14.d. from
   7.30 a.m.)   the direction of LE CATELET.
   The following localities were shelled during the day:–
   LITTLE PRIEL FARM – MALASSISE FARM (4 21 cm. shells from LE CATELET direction) – 12 copse – 13 copse – "G" "H" Posts and X.21.d.

   (b) *Movement.*

   11.15 a.m. 6 men came out of the Southern house of LA TERRIERE, one carrying a white flag, which they hoisted. This flag was taken down twice in the first five minutes, and put up again each time. It remained up, after 5 of the men had gone, until 12.45 p.m., when the remaining man took it down and carried it away.
   11.45 a.m. What appeared to be a large explosion was seen in RANCOURT FARM.
   2.15 p.m. A fatigue party of 28 men seen going W. down BEAUREVOIR – GOUY road.
   7.15 p.m. About 200 men reported moving W. by sections down BEAUREVOIR – GOUY road, in marching order.
   The usual movement seen in the vicinity of LA TERRIERE & FRANQUE WOOD.

   (c) *Aviation.*

   Only 2 enemy machines attempted to cross our lines. They withdrew under the fire of our A.A. guns.

3. **Hostile Defences.**

   (a) *Work and New trenches.*

   A reconnaissance, carried out from the sector on our left, revealed new enemy work on the S. side of CANAL WOOD about X.24.a.2.9.

   this

this trench appeared to run S.E. from the edge of the WOOD for about 25^x.

    (b) <u>Wire</u>.

About 150^x of new wire is reported to have been put up by the enemy last night about X.30.c.6.2. - near where the coils of wire were seen yesterday, lying behind the trenches.

                                  Sd. W.P.Browne, Captain,
                                        General Staff,
13th. June, 1917.   3rd. Cavalry Division.

C O R R I G E N D U M.
****

Reference yesterday's Summary 3 (1) for X.32.c.6.0., please read X.30.c.6.0.

                    ****

3rd CAVALRY DIVISION INTELLIGENCE SUMMARY, for 24 hours from 8 a.m. 13th to 8 a.m. 14th June, 1917.

1. **OPERATIONS ON DIVISIONAL FRONT.**

   (a) **Patrols.**
   (i) An Officers' patrol went out from No.1 Post to reconnoitre the enemy's wire at X.23.d.8½.4½. When they were within 200x of this point, a M.G. opened fire on them. They believed it to be firing from X.23.d.8½.4½. They altered their course and proceeded another 100x in a N.E. direction. They heard a small party wiring at about X.24.a.0.0.
   (ii) A patrol went out from No. 3 Post to reconnoitre the enemy's wire at X.24.a.2.4. They heard a small wiring party at work at this point; M.G. fire from the North of CANAL WOOD, and the rising moon compelled the patrol to return. No movement was heard in CANAL WOOD.

   (b) **Our Artillery.**
   We shelled the enemy's front lines in X.24.a., X.30.a. and F.6.a. at intervals during the day.
   The following localities were also shelled by us :-
   VENDHUILE, MACQUINCOURT FARM, OSSUS WOOD, S.22.d., OSSUS, S.14.a. and CANAL WOOD.

2. **HOSTILE ATTITUDE AND ACTIVITY.**

   (a) **Artillery.**
   Hostile Artillery was more active than formerly against our front system.
   (i) About 70 shells were fired at PETIT PRIEL FARM during the day - mostly 77 mm from the VENDHUILE direction.
   (ii) <u>9-25 a.m.</u> 12 77 mm shells were fired into X.29 from the direction of A.17.
   (iii) <u>11-0 a.m. to 12 noon.</u> F.5. and X.29 were shelled with 77 mm's from LE CATELET direction.
   (iv) <u>12 noon.</u> Enemy shelled VILLERS GUISLAIN. The gun appeared to fire from FRANQUE WOOD.
   (v) X.21.a.7.9. and X.22.c. shelled with 4.2's and 77 mm's from 2-30 p.m. - 45 shells were fired.

   (b) **Movement.**
   Enemy transport could be heard at midnight crossing the Canal near CANAL WOOD.
   Throughout the day, small parties of men and horse-drawn traffic were observed moving in both directions on the BEAUREVOIR - GOUY Road, past BELLEVUE FARM.
   An enemy observer has been seen nightly at about 7 p.m. in the trench about F.6.a.6.7. After we had put 4 shells on to this point, he was not seen again.

   (c) **Aviation.**
   <u>8-0 a.m.</u> 5 enemy machines flew over our lines for 5 minutes. They were engaged by A.A. Guns and automatic rifles and withdrew to the North.
   <u>8-45 p.m.</u> Enemy machine flew over BIRDCAGE and L and M Posts and withdrew under heavy fire from A.A. Guns.
   <u>9-45 p.m.</u> One machine crossed our line and came on until nearly over EPEHY. After 10 minutes he turned East again and disappeared.

3. HOSTILE DEFENCES.

(1) Wire.

Sentries in the BIRDCAGE report hearing the sounds of stakes being driven into the ground from their right front to OSSUS WOOD during the night.

Observers report that the enemy is wiring along the trench from F.6.a.4.9. to F.6.a.9.0., and that material is brought up from VENDHUILE to A.1.b.6.7., where there is presumed to be a Dump.

At 2 p.m. yesterday, a working party of about 12 men were seen wiring in front of trench at S.9.c.9.2. for one hour.

4. NEIGHBOURING DIVISIONS.

Constant movement throughout the day is reported to and from BONABUS FARM along the track to S.11.a.6.4. From the amount of traffic, it is suspected that the Farm is used as H.Q.

5. GENERAL NEWS.

London, 13th June, 1917.

Hostile aeroplanes raided LONDON today, about noon. One bomb fell in a Railway Station, hitting an incoming train, eleven persons being killed and seventeen injured. Another bomb fell on a school, killing 10 and injuring about 50 children.

A number of warehouses were damaged and fires were caused. Up to the present the number of casualties caused in the LONDON area is 41 killed and 121 injured. The raid over LONDON lasted about 15 minutes. The raiders were engaged in combat, but the results at present are uncertain.

The KING has visited the affected area.

(sd) W.P. BROWNE, Captain,
14th June, 1917.   G.S., 3rd Cavalry Division.

3rd. Cavalry Division Intelligence Summary for 24 hours -

8 a.m. 14th. to 8 a.m. 15th. June, 1917.

1. **Operations on Divisional Front.**

   (a) **Our patrols.**

   (i) At 11 p.m. a patrol went out to reconnoitre a suspected enemy listening post at the S.W. end of OSSUS WOOD. 4 of the enemy were heard wispering and moving about near a tree, which stands just S. of the WOOD about X.29.b.5.3., where a small pit can be seen. This is therefore, concluded to be the L.P., which is occupied at night.

   (b) **Our artillery.**

   We shelled VENDHUILE during the day - also the trenches in the following areas - A.4.a, F.6.a., X.30, X.23.b.
   The enemy's trenches in S.26.a.1.7., and S.20.a.4.1., were fired at effectively, with aeroplane observation, - between 5 p.m. and 6 p.m.

2. **Hostile Attitude and Activity.**

   (a) **Artillery.**

   7.15.a.m. to 9.30 a.m. } 16 77mm. shells were fired into PETIT PRIEL and "H" Post, from the LA TERRIERE direction.

   9 a.m. to 10.20 a.m. } 27 4.2's were fired into 13 COPSE from LA TERRIERE direction.

   9.30 a.m. to 10.15 a.m. } 30 4.2's fell in F.9. - coming from BASKET WOOD direction.

   11 a.m. to 11.15 a.m. } Enemy put 17 4.2's into PETIT PRIEL and "G" Post - from BASKET WOOD direction.

   11.a.m. to 12 noon. } 20 4.2's fell in X.20.a., apparently fired from HONNECOURT.

   Slight shelling of the whole of the forward area was reported during the morning, in addition to the above.
   A 77 mm. gun is reported to be firing from a new position near BONY.
   This gun appeared to be registering on our trenches in F.4.b. and F.5.c.

   (b) **Movement.**

   General.

   (i) 11.30 a.m. 4 men were seen at S.21.a.9.8., observing our lines through field-glasses.
   (ii) 12.30 p.m. A working party of about 20 men seen, apparently wiring-A.3.b.8.2.
   (iii) Considerable movement was observed throughout the day in S.2?

   in the HINDENBURG LINE.

   Westward.

Westward Movement — BEAUREVOIR — GOUY road.

(iv). 7.15 p.m. Several small parties seen moving West from BELLEVUE FARM.

(v) 7.27 p.m. 100 - 150 men, in marching order, were seen marching West. from BELLEVUE FARM, in 2 parties at about 50^x interval.
This party was followed by several more men, marching in two's and three's, until after 8 p.m.

(vi) 8.15 p.m. 2 motor cars and 2 lorries seen going W. from BELLEVUE FARM.

LE CATELET — PUTNEY road.

(i) 7.30 p.m. 10 men marched towards PUTNEY in half-sections at 50^x interval, followed by one platoon in close order.
Motor traffic was also observed on this road.

3. Hostile Defences.

(a) Work and New Trenches.

(i) 2 men are reported to have been seen working on a small post (a sniper's nest ?) at X.23.c.8.0. This requires confirmation.

(ii) The enemy's sap, running from W.S.W. from X.30.a.4.6. (vide 3rd. Cav. Div. Summary 11th. June, para 3 (iii)) is shown by recent aeroplane photographs to have been prolonged in a S.W. direction. It now runs out as far as X.30.a.2.3.

(b) Wire.

The wire in front of the enemy's front line from the KNOLL Northwards has been continued to join the wire of the VENDHUILE - OSSUS WOOD Line about X.30.c.45.65. This is confirmed by Air photos, taken on 13th. June.

(c) Demolitions.

11.43 p.m. a fire broke out in RANCOURT FARM, followed 2 minutes later by an explosion.

4. Hostile Organization.

(a) A small dump of between 30 to 40 boxes (of ammunition ?) was seen at S.27.c.9.3.

5. Miscellaneous.

3 Mowing-machines were seen at work just W. of LA TERRIERE during the afternoon.

6. Late News. Operations.

At 1.30 a.m., an enemy patrol attempted to bomb a wiring party in front of No. 1 Post. They were driven off by our covering party.

15th. June, 1917.

Sd. W.P.Brunne, Capt,
General Staff,
3rd. Cavalry Division.

ANNEXE to 3rd CAVALRY DIVISION INTELLIGENCE SUMMARY,

14th June, 1917.

CALENDAR FOR JUNE, 1917.

TIMES CALCULATED FOR FOURTH ARMY FRONT AND SUMMER TIME.

S U N.			M O O N.			
Day of month.	Rises.	Sets.	Day of month.	Rises.	Sets.	Phase.
12.	4.40.	8.53.	12.	0.36am	1.4pm	Last Qr.
13.	4.40.	8.54.	13.	0.57.	2.24.	
14.	4.40.	8.55.	14.	1.16.	3.43.	
15.	4.39.	8.55.	15.	1.38.	5. 1.	
16.	4.39.	8.56.	16.	2. 5.	6. 1.	
17.	4.39.	8.56.	17.	2.38.	7.25.	
18.	4.39.	8.56.	18.	3.22.	8.26.	
19.	4.39.	8.57.	19.	4.15.	9.14.	New Mn.
20.	4.39.	8.57.	20.	5.17.	9.49.	
21.	4.39.	8.57.	21.	6.22.	10.19.	
22.	4.40.	8.58.	22.	7.30.	10.42.	
23.	4.40.	8.58.	23.	8.37.	11. 1.	
24.	4.40.	8.58.	24.	9.46.	11.18.	
25.	4.41.	8.58.	25.	10.50.	11.35.	
26.	4.41.	8.58.	26.	11.56.	11.51.	
27.	4.41.	8.58.	27.	1.4pm		First Qr.
28.	4.42.	8.58.	28.	2.12.	0. 7am	
29.	4.42.	8.58.	29.	3.23.	0.25.	
30.	4.43.	8.57.	30.	4.37.	0.47.	

Note: At certain times the Moon rises on one day and sets on the next; this is indicated by arrows connecting the rising time with the following setting time.

3rd. Cavalry Division Fortnightly Summary
Period ending June, 15th. 1917.
==*=*=*=*=*=*=*=*=*=*

1. **PRISONERS.**

   No prisoners were captured.

2. **OPERATIONS.**

   (a) General.

   The enemy's attitude has been a purely defensive one. Every night, patrols have been up to the wire of his front line in several places and, though they find the enemy very much on the alert, no hostile patrol has been met with on these ventures.

   (b) Bombing Enterprises.

   The only enemy patrol, which has been encountered was on the night 14th/15th, when a small bombing patrol attacked a working party on the night 14th/15th, but were driven off by our covering party.

3. Air Activity and Places Bombed.

   (a) Air Activity.

   Hostile Air Activity has remained normal - not more than 2 or 3 enemy machines fly over our trenches daily.

   (b) Places Bombed.

   No bombing enterprises were undertaken by the enemy in our area.

4. Enemy Work.

   (a) N. of OSSUS WOOD, the enemy appears to have done practically no work on his front line trenches and it is doubtful if this line is held at all during the day-time.

   (b) OSSUS WOOD and S. of it, the enemy has made several additions to his defences, as under:-

   (i) A sap has been run out W.S.W. from the VENDHUILE - OSSUS WOOD Line in X.30.a.4.6. to X.30.a.2.3.
   (ii) From X.30.a.4.7. in the above line, he has connected up a line of shell holes and has made a traversed fire-trench, running to the S. edge of OSSUS WOOD in X.30.a.2.8.
   (iii) This line is almost certainly prolonged Northwards by a trench which runs across the wood from X.30. a. 2.8. to X.24.c.0.0.
   (iv) The line through F.6.a. is now prolonged Northwards beyond the PETIT PRIEL - VENDHUILE road to about X.30.c.6.4., where it disappears over the sky-line. This line is probably being connected up with the VENDHUILE - OSSUS WOOD Line in X.30.c.7.7. The wire of these 2 lines is shown as already joined up in Air Photos, taken 13th. June.

   Enemy wiring parties have been frequently reported in this line.

   (c) Small working parties are continually seen in the HINDENBURG LINE opposite our whole front.
   New work is frequently reported in S.21.central.

(d)

(d) General.

Small wiring parties and evidence of fresh wire are continually reported - out patrol activity appears to have made the enemy anxious to improve his entanglements.

Sd. W.P.Browne, Captain,

15th. June, 1917.   General Staff, 3rd. Cavalry Division.

3rd CAVALRY DIVISION INTELLIGENCE SUMMARY for 24 hours

8 a.m. 15th to 8 a.m. 16th June, 1917.

1. OPERATIONS ON DIVISIONAL FRONT.
   (a) Our Patrols.
   (i) An officers' patrol went out at 11-0 p.m., from the BIRDCAGE to reconnoitre towards the enemy's sap in X.30.a. Patrol got out 50^x beyond our wire to about X.30.a.2.2. From this point they saw an enemy covering party about 20^x away. They could hear a working party about 50^x beyond in a N.E. direction - they were working very quickly. They heard transport, which was thought to be on the road, about X.30.a.7.4.
   (ii) A strong Officers' patrol went out at 10-40 p.m. from X.17.d. to about X.18.c.5.9. They found no sign of the enemy or of any work, but report Very Lights were being fired from about X.17.b. Central.

   Patrol then attempted to reconnoitre CANAL WOOD, but could get no further than X.18.c.1.2., owing to the number of Very Lights which the enemy were putting up from about X.30.a.5.9. They returned at 1-45 a.m.

   No M.G. was firing in, or across, the area traversed. They report considerable work going on about X.18.c.5.3.

   (b) Our Artillery.
   9-30 a.m. Our 18 pdrs. shelled FRANQUE WOOD.
   During the day our 13 pdrs. shelled the enemy's trenches at the following points :- X.24.a. and c. and X.30.a. and c. and F.6.a.

2. HOSTILE ATTITUDE AND ACTIVITY.

   (a) Artillery.
   9-30 a.m. to 10-30 a.m. and at 12-45 p.m., TOMBOIS FARM shelled with 11 rounds 77 mm from the direction of VENDHUILE.
   9-45 a.m. F.4.a. shelled with 15 rounds 77 mm from the direction of LE CATELET.
   10-30 a.m. The neighbourhood of TOMBOIS FARM shelled with 17 rounds 4.2 from the direction of VENDHUILE.
   10-30 a.m. and 11-30 a.m. PETIT PRIEL FARM was shelled with 4.2. from the direction of LE CATELET.
   5-15 - 5-30 p.m. MALASSISE FARM shelled with 11 rounds 4.2 from the direction of LA TERRIERE.
   The Quarry in X.29.d.3.3. was shelled at intervals during the afternoon.

   (b) Movement.
   8-30 a.m. 3 men seen at A.1.a.5.6. apparently observing our positions. They were using field glasses.
   12-45 p.m. 5 men were seen in trench about X.30.c.5.4. This appears to be an O.P. One man seemed to be observing while the others dug.
   6-20 p.m. 5 men seen digging a trench in S.26.d. Between 7-0 and 8-0 p.m. motor traffic in both directions was observed on the CATELET - PUTNEY Road.
   During the day, many instances of one man pointing out the country to another were observed. This may indicate a relief.

   (c) Aviation.
   9-0 p.m. A hostile machine flew over our lines.

3/

3.   **Hostile Defences.**

   Machine Guns.

   At 2.45 p.m. a M.G. fired at one of our aeroplanes from FRANQUE WOOD.

4.   **Neighbouring Divisions.**
   Identifications.
   A prisoner belonging to the 124th. I.R. was captured this morning in X.5.c. From this it would appear that this Regiment is holding the most Northerly Sector of the 27th. Divisional Front.

16th. June, 1917.
            Sd. W.P. Browne, Capt,
            General Staff,
            3rd. Cavalry Division.

3rd. Cavalry Division Intelligence Summary for period -

8 a.m. 16th. to 8 a.m. 17th. June, 1917.

1. Operations on Divisional Front.

(a) Our Patrols.

(i) A patrol of 1 N.C.O. and 3 men went out at 11.15 p.m. from No. 2 Post to reconnoitre a suspected M.G. emplacement reported to be at X.23.b.8.2. The patrol went out to SOLITARY TREE due East of No. 2 Post and proceeded in a South Easterly direction for about 150 yards: from this point the N.C.O. went on alone for another 50 yards in the same direction when he saw a dark object in front of him which he took to be a small emplacement. He heard a voice call out "FELDWEBEL" (Sergt-Major) and 3 shots were fired in his direction but he was not challenged. Immediately afterwards a M.G. fired a short burst to his left. He then returned.

(ii) An officers patrol went out from the BIRDCAGE at 11.15 p.m. There were no sounds of work or other signs of occupation of the new sap. An enemy working party was heard at X.30.a.3.8. On the way back they found what appeared to be a snipers nest and the advance patrol reported the flight of three occupants. This was confirmed by three tracks discovered in the grass. The patrol returned at 2.15 a.m.

(b) Our Artillery.

Between 9 a.m. and 10 a.m., and again between 5 p.m. and 6 p.m. our 13 prs. shelled the enemy positions in F.6.a.

During the afternoon our 4.5 hows. put 50 rounds into X.29.b.5.5. where hostile M.G's were suspected; they also shelled S.19.d.1.5. and KINGSTON QUARRY.

5 p.m. our 13 prs. shelled a house at S.27.a.2.6. (suspected to be an O.P) with 11 rounds. Direct hits were obtained.

2. Hostile Attitude and Activity.

(a) Artillery.

8 a.m. - 8.20 a.m. PETIT PRIEL FARM, F.4.c., and No. 12 COPSE were shelled with 4.2 from the direction of LE CATELET.

8.40 a.m. "L" Post was shelled with 20 rounds 5.9 at intervals of 1 minute from the direction of LA PANNERIE.

CATELET VALLEY - TOMBOIS VALLEY and TOMBOIS FARM were shelled intermittently during the day.

A considerable number of blinds were reported yesterday.

8.57 a.m. H.Post was shelled with 6 rounds 77mm. from the direction of LA TERRIERE.

(b) Movement.

Movement on the roads behind the enemy's positions was above normal.

At 7.45 a.m. a party of 15 to 20 men were observed on the FRANQUEVILLE - LA TERRIERE road at S.14.a.9.5. proceeding in the direction of LA TERRIERE.

In the evening between 7.30 p.m. and 8.30 p.m. 12 small parties of 6 or 8 men were observed moving on the BEAUREVOIR - GOUY main road at intervals of 200 yards in the direction of GOUY. These were followed by a party of 50 men marching in the same direction.

At 3.45 p.m. two parachutes descended from a balloon behind LA TERRIERE. One descended fairly straight the other was blown in the direction of RANCOURT FARM. The balloon was then hauled down. This is the first time this balloon has been up for several days and this may have been an experiment with dummy men.

A certain amount of movement was observed throughout the day on the HINDENBURG LINE.

Aviation.

8.50 a.m. 1 E.A. crossed our lines but returned very quickly.
6 p.m. 3 E.A. crossed our lines flying very high.
The A.A. Gun which usually fires from the direction of HONNECOURT seems to have moved further South.

3. Hostile Defences.

New work. The enemy appear to be sapping back from their advanced trench at F.6.a.9.4.

Wire.

The wire at X.30.a.4.5. has been strengthened and coils of wire can be seen lying at this point.

Loophole.

A loophole can be seen at A.1.a.2.4.

Late News.

A hostile aeroplane was brought down in flames this morning East of HONNECOURT.

                                                    Sd. W.R.Brandt, Lt.
                                                      for General Staff,
17th. June, 1917.   3rd. Cavalry Division.

3rd CAVALRY DIVISION INTELLIGENCE SUMMARY for 24 hours

from 8 a.m. 17th to 8 a.m. 18th June, 1917.

1. OPERATIONS ON DIVISIONAL FRONT.

(a) Our Patrols.

(i) A fighting patrol went out last night to the enemy's sap in X.30.a. after a short bombardment by Stokes Mortars. As our patrol approached the trench, about 12 of the enemy jumped out over the back of the trench and lay down in the open. Both sides opened fire, and our patrol entered the trench and threw bombs at the enemy, four of which were seen to have good effect, bursting in the midst of the Germans. Our party eventually withdrew without any casualties. The sap appeared to be 2 feet deep. Full details have not yet been received.

(ii) A strong Officer's patrol was also sent to reconnoitre the enemy's front line about X.30 Central, where the enemy was suspected of constructing another sap. About X.30.c.5.9. they discovered a converted shell-hole, which they took to be a forward M.G. emplacement. As our patrol approached, 3 Germans crawled out of it to a post about 15^x in rear. Our patrol was challenged and then fired upon. The enemy post was just in front of their wire. It was an entrenched position and seemed strongly held. The enemy in it were soon reinforced. These men moved across the open, and it is, therefore, presumed that the post and the M.G. emplacement in front of it are both isolated positions, and not connected by a sap to the fire-trench.

(iii) An Officer's patrol went out last night from No. 1 Post to reconnoitre an enemy post in X.23.d.2½.5½. where the enemy had been seen digging during the day. The post, which was unoccupied, though there were evidences of recent occupation, was about 6 yards long, running approximately North to South. It was about 4' 6" deep and 2' 6" wide, with a small covered shelter at either end. The floor was boarded. There was a piece of thin wire leading from the S. end towards the SUNKEN ROAD for 60 yards. This was loose and had, evidently, not been in use. The patrol proceeded as far as the road in X.23.d.5.1. and then returned. No signs of the enemy were encountered.

(b) Our Artillery.

Throughout the day, our Artillery shelled the enemy's front line North and South of OSSUS WOOD.

2. HOSTILE ATTITUDE AND ACTIVITY.

(a) Artillery.

Between 10 a.m. and 10-30 a.m. "L" Post, CATELET COPSE, 13 COPSE and PETIT PRIEL FARM were shelled with 4.2 cm and 77 mm.

From 11 a.m. to 2-20 p.m. RONSSOY WOOD was shelled with 8" from the direction of MT. ST. MARTIN, about 50 rounds were fired.

12-15 p.m. - 12-35 p.m. "L" Post shelled with 20 rounds 4.2".

4-50 p.m. 6 rounds of 5.9" fired from the direction of BASKET WOOD, fell in the neighbourhood of LEMPIRE.

(b) Movement.

(i) Considerable movement was observed during the day in the enemy front line South of OSSUS WOOD.

(ii) The usual working parties were seen on the HINDENBURG LINE.

(iii) No movement on the roads was reported.

(c)/

(c) Aviation.

During the morning, enemy air activity was above normal. At 9-0 a.m. an air fight took place between a Squadron of our battle planes and an unknown number of E.A. One E.A. was brought down in flames, falling about S.20.

At 12-5 p.m. one E.A. flew over our lines for 10 minutes.

At 3-0 p.m. 8 E.A. crossed our lines flying very high, returning ½ an hour later.

3. HOSTILE DEFENCES.

(a) New Work.
Holes covered with what appears to be netting, have been dug in a field at S.20.c.6.4.; possibly Snipers' nests.

(b) M.G's.
(i) A M.G. has been located approximately in S.14.c.
(ii) A M.G. emplacement is suspected at A.3.c.8.2.
(iii) A M.G. post is located at the foot of a big tree in X.23.b.5.9.

(c) Listening Post.
There is an enemy Listening Post at X.23.b.6.7.

4. NEIGHBOURING DIVISIONS.
Patrol. The Division on our left reports that a patrol reconnoitred the Crater in X.17.b. and found it unoccupied. The Crater is really a small chalk quarry just alongside the road.

M.G. The Division on our right reports the flash of a M.G. from the small bushes 100 yards due N. of LONE TREE (A.7.d.85.70.).

(Sd) W.R. BRANDT, Lieut.,

18th June, 1917. for G.S., 3rd Cavalry Division.

3rd. Cavalry Division Intelligence Summary for period -

8 a.m. 18th. to 8 a.m. 19th. June, 1917.

1. Operations on Divisional Front.

ARTILLERY.

During the day our 13 pdrs. and 4.5 Hows. shelled VENDHUILE and the enemy's first line trenches North and South of OSSUS WOOD.

At 4.30 p.m. our 13 pdrs. shelled the new enemy post in X.23.d.2½.5½. (reported in 3rd. Cav. Div. Intelligence Summary 1.a.3, for 17th. - 18th. inst.) Several direct hits were obtained.

At 5.30 p.m. our 13 pdrs. shelled the OSSUS WOOD - VENDHUILE road in S.25.d.

2. Hostile Attitude and Activity.

(a) Artillery.

8 a.m. No. 12 COPSE shelled with 15 rounds 77 mm. from the direction of LA TERRIERE.

Between 8.30 and 9.30 a.m. our positions running between "L" Post and "G" Post, were shelled with 4.2. from the direction of LA TERRIERE and with 77 mm. from the direction of LE CATELET.

At 9.40 a.m. the BIRDCAGE was shelled with 20 rounds of 77 mm. from the direction of LA TERRIERE.

Throughout the day CATELET VALLEY - PETIT PRIEL FARM and TOMBOIS VALLEY and FARM were shelled intermittently.

A hostile battery was observed in action near the road at S.9.a.4.2.

(b) Movement.

Throughout the morning men were seen in the trench at F.6.a.6.5. observing our positions through field-glasses.

Movement was observed all day in the trench in X.30.c.

At 6 p.m. a man was seen observing our line through glasses from a hole at S.2.b.0.6.

The usual amount of digging etc., was observed going on on the HINDENBURG LINE.

3. Aviation.

11.30 a.m. 1 E.A. crossed our lines flying very high .
5 p.m. 2 E.A. manoeuvred over our lines in X.17.a. and c.
4 a.m. 1 E.A. flew low over "H" Post in a northerly direction.

4. Hostile Defences.

Work.

What appear to be two concreted emplacements can be seen at about S.21.d.2.8.

5. Neighbouring Divisions.

M.Gs. are reported to be active from the S.W. corner of HONNECOURT WOOD.

Sd. W.R.Brandt. Lieut,

19th. June, 1917.   for G.S. 3rd. Cavalry Division.

3rd CAVALRY DIVISION INTELLIGENCE SUMMARY FOR 24 HOURS,

8 a.m. 19th to 8 a.m. 20th June, 1917.

1. OPERATIONS ON DIVISIONAL FRONT.

Artillery.
Between 9-30 a.m. and 10-30 a.m., and again in the afternoon and evening, our 4.5" Howrs shelled VENDHUILE and KINGSTON QUARRIES. During the day our 18 pdrs shelled the following places :- OSSUS WOOD, Line of dug-outs in S.20.a. and LA TERRIERE.

2. HOSTILE ATTITUDE AND ACTIVITY.

(a) Artillery.
(i) The enemy's artillery was active during the morning; an unusual number of "blinds" are reported.
(ii) Our positions lying between CATELET VALLEY and TOMBOIS FARM were shelled intermittently throughout the day with 4.2 cm and 77 mm.
(iii) Between 9-50 a.m. and 10-30 a.m. a 13 cm gun, firing from the direction of VENDHUILE, shelled PETIT PRIEL FARM with 20 rounds, of which half were "blind".

(b) Movement.
(i) 9-30 a.m. A working party was heard on the West of CANAL WOOD; one man was seen on the edge of the Wood.
(ii) 3-0 p.m. 2 men seen in hole just East of the road at X.23.b.5.5., observing our positions through glasses.
(iii) A good deal of movement was seen in the front line trenches S. of OSSUS WOOD. Two periscopes were put up in the trench in X.30.d., and shortly afterwards our positions opposite were shelled.
(iv) The usual working parties were observed on the HINDENBURG LINE.
(v) In the evening, large parties of men and transport were seen entering VENDHUILE from LE CATELET.

(c) Aviation.
E.A. activity was below normal. The enemy seems to be making less use of his A.A. guns than usual.

3. HOSTILE DEFENCES.

(a) New Work.
Signs of fresh digging can be seen between F.6.a.6.1. and F.3.a.7.2.

(b) Wire.
(i) New wire has been put up about 20 yards in front of the German front line at X.30.c.4.3. near the road; it is trip wire.
(ii) A stake or post is visible in the enemy's wire in front of the new enemy sap opposite the BIRDCAGE.

(c) Machine Guns.
A M.G. was reported firing up PIGEON RAVINE at 11 p.m.

20th June, 1917.   (Sd) W.R. BRANDT, Lieut.,
                                    for G.S., 3rd Cavalry Division.

CORRIGENDUM.
Reference 3rd Cav. Div. Summary for 18th-19th instant, para. 2 (b) 3, for S.2.b.0.6. read S.21.b.0.6.

3rd. Cavalry Division Intelligence Summary for period -
8 a.m. 20th. to 8 a.m. 21st. June, 1917.

1. **Operations on Divisional Front.**

   (i) <u>Artillery.</u>

   Between 8.20 a.m. and 11.30 a.m. our 13 pdrs. and 4.5 Hows. shelled OSSUS WOOD and VENDHUILE and the enemy positions lying between those places.
   9.30 a.m. our 18 pdrs. effectively dispersed a party which was collecting on the road at S.15.b.1.9.
   12.15 p.m. our 13 pdrs. shelled the houses in S.29.a.1.9.
   In the evening our 13 pdrs. shelled the enemy trenches North of OSSUS WOOD.

   (ii) <u>Hostile Attitude and Activity.</u>

   (a) <u>Artillery.</u>

   (1) Enemy artillery was unusually active during the day the greater part of the shooting being done with 4.2.cm.
   During the earlier part of the day he seemed to be registering the BIRDCAGE Area.
   (2) Between 8 a.m. and 10 a.m. and from 11.30 to 12 noon "G" and "H" Posts and PETIT PRIEL FARM were shelled with 4.2 from the direction of LA TERRIERE.
   (3) Between 2.30 and 3 p.m. the QUARRY in X.29.d. was shelled from the same direction.
   (4) Between 8.a.m. and 8.15 a.m. a 13 cm. H.V. Gun put 30 shells in F.5.a. from the direction of LA PANNERIE, 50% of these were "blind".

   (b) <u>Movement.</u>

   (1) The enemy trenches opposite the BIRDCAGE were seen to be occupied during the day.
   (2) Men were seen observing our positions through glasses from holes at S.26.a.2.5. and S.20.b.5.5. The two occupants of S.20.b.5.5. were relieved every two hours.
   (3) A certain amount of movement in CANAL WOOD is reported.
   (4) A party of six men were seen in front of the German wire opposite the BIRDCAGE apparently taking ground measurements.
   (5) A working party was observed in S.28.a. apparently putting up an overhead telegraph line.
   (6) A considerable amount of traffic, both troop and transport was observed in both directions on the GOUY - BEAUREVOIR and GOUY - VILLERS OUTREAUX roads.

   (c) <u>Aviation.</u>

   Very little E.A. activity. In the evening 6 E.A. approached our lines from the N.E. and returned in the same direction.

   (d) <u>Fires.</u>

   A large fire was seen in VILLERS OUTREAUX and another in AUBENCHEUL.

21st. June, 1917.   Sd. W.R. BRANDT. Lieut.,
                        for G.S., 3rd. Cavalry Division.

3rd CAVALRY DIVISION INTELLIGENCE SUMMARY for 24 hours

from 8 a.m. 21st to 8 a.m. 22nd June, 1917.

1. **OPERATIONS ON DIVISIONAL FRONT.**

   The enemy attempted a raid on the BIRDCAGE at 1-15 a.m. The raid was completely broken by our fire and none of the enemy succeeded in reaching our trenches; 10 enemy dead have been counted on our wire, and 3 wounded Germans were captured, two of whom have since died. Full details have not yet been received.
   (b) Artillery.
   Between 9-20 a.m. and 4-0 p.m. our 13 pdrs and 4.2" Howrs shelled the enemy's front line North and South of OSSUS WOOD; OSSUS WOOD; and VENDHUILE. 294 rounds were fired.

2. **HOSTILE ATTITUDE AND ACTIVITY.**
   (a) Artillery.
   8-0 a.m. TOMBOIS VALLEY shelled with 30 rounds 4.2 cm from the direction of VENDHUILE.
   9-20 a.m. No. 12 COPSE shelled with 10 rounds 77 mm from the direction of VENDHUILE.
   10-0 a.m. PETIT PRIEL FARM shelled with 20 rounds 4.2 cm from the direction of LA TERRIERE.
   3-15 – 4-0 p.m. The BIRDCAGE and PETIT PRIEL FARM were shelled with 4.2 cm.
   (b) Movement.
   (i) Observers were again seen at S.26.a.2.5. and X.23.b.8.25 (wrongly reported in yesterday's Summary as S.20.b.5.5.)
   (ii) One man was seen at A.1.b.4.4.; probably observing.
   (iii) The usual amount of traffic was observed on the GOUY - BEAUREVOIR and GOUY - VILLERS OUTREAUX Roads. A party of about 12 men, in marching order, were seen marching Northwards on the BEAUREVOIR - VILLERS OUTREAUX Road at 11-30 a.m.
   (c) Aviation.
   (i) 8-30 a.m. 1 E.A. appeared over our lines; it was fired on by our A.A. guns and returned in a N.E. direction.
   (ii) An enemy observation balloon ascended and descended over BONABUS FARM at intervals during the day. Enemy Artillery activity from the direction of VENDHUILE is reported contemporaneously with the ascent of this balloon.

3. **ENEMY DEFENCES.**
   Work. Signs of fresh digging can be seen at S.20.b.5.9.

4. **ENEMY ORGANISATION.**
   Demolitions.
   At 6-30 p.m. a large volume of smoke as though from an explosion, was seen in VILLERS OUTREAUX.

5. **DISTRIBUTION OF ENEMY's FORCES.**
   The following identification has been established :-
   3rd Res. Div.
   2nd R.I.R. ... VENDHUILE Area ... 3 prisoners ... normal.
   Two of these prisoners have since died, and the third, who is very badly wounded, has not yet been examined. The prisoners had no pay books or other marks of identification on their persons, with the exception of one envelope which bears the address "5th Company, 2nd R.I.R.

22nd June, 1917.
(Sd) W.R. BRANDT, Lieut,
for G.S., 3rd Cavalry Division.

CORRIGENDUM.
Reference 3rd Cav. Div. Summary for 20th-21st inst, para. 2 (b) 2, for S.20.b.5.5. read X.23.b.8.25.

3rd. Cavalry Division Intelligence Summary for period -
8 a.m. 22nd. to 8 a.m. 23rd. June, 1917.

1. **Operations on Divisional Front.**

    (a) A report on the enemy raid on the BIRDCAGE on the morning of the 22nd. inst. is annexed.

    (b) Artillery.

    3.15 p.m. - 3.30 p.m. our 13 pdrs. shelled X.24.c.5.6. - X.24.c.5.9 and X.18.d.8.2.
    5.10 p.m. our 13 pdrs. fired 18 rounds into OSSUS WOOD.

2. **Enemy Attitude and Activity.**

    (a) Artillery.

    8.30 a.m. TARGELLE VALLEY shelled with 15 rounds 77 mm. from the direction of LA TERRIERE.
    10.15 - 10.30 a.m. TOMBOIS FARM shelled with 7 rounds 77 mm. from the direction of VENDHUILE.
    1 p.m. X.20.b.5.5. was shelled with 3 rounds 77 mm. from the direction of HONNECOURT.
    5.10 p.m. X.27.b. was shelled with 6 rounds 77 mm.
    5.15 p.m. Our positions in X.23. received 7 rounds of 4.2 cm. from the direction of KINGSTON QUARRY.

    (b) Movement.

    During the day observers were again seen observing our lines through glasses from X.23.b.8.25. and S.26.a.2.5.
    1.20 p.m. 6 men were seen leaving a tin hut at S.27.c.7.2. and entering a trench at S.27.c.9.1. 7 others came out of this trench and entered the hut.
    3.5 p.m. 2 men emerged from hole on top of bank S.20.c.1.9. one of these men carried field-glasses and the other apparently had a map.
    5.40 p.m. men seen observing our line with glasses from S.21.a.9.8.
    The usual working parties could be seen on the HINDENBURG LINE.
    A considerable amount of transport was observed throughout the day on the GOUY - BEAUREVOIR road going in both directions.

    (c) Aviation.

    There was very little E.A. activity yesterday, in the evening 6 E.A. approached our lines but did not cross them.

3. **Hostile Defences.**

    (a) Work. A newly built airline can be seen running from VENDHUILE on the crest of hill 130 in S.28.b. A working party were se working on this line on the 19th. inst., and it is since then that the 13 cm. H.V. Gun. has been active; this line may possibly be the battery to O.P. line, and the gun itself is probably in action behind the hill.

    (c) Miscellaneous. A searchlight is often seen from just N.E. of LA TERRIERE at about midnight.

23rd. June, 1917.

Sd. W.R. BRANDT, Lieut,
for G.S., 3rd. Cavalry Division.

3rd CAVALRY DIVISION INTELLIGENCE SUMMARY FOR 24 HOURS 8 a.m. 23rd to 8 a.m. 24th JUNE, 1917.

1. OPERATIONS ON DIVISIONAL FRONT.

   (a) Patrols.
   A Listening Patrol sent out from the S.E. end of the BIRDCAGE at dark reported seeing a small enemy wiring party at work in about X.30.c.5.6. Further to the South, a large working party could be heard.

   (b) Artillery.
   During the day, our Artillery shelled the following localities:- LA TERRIERE; FFAFQUE WOOD and the enemy's line running between CANAL WOOD and VENDHUILE.

2. ENEMY ATTITUDE AND ACTIVITY.

   (a) Artillery.
   Between 10 a.m. and 1 p.m., the neighbourhood of TARGELLE Valley and PIGEON RAVINE was shelled with 77 mm and 4.2 cm from the direction of HONNECOURT.

   (b) Movement.
   Between 9-30 a.m. and 2-0 p.m., the holes in X.23.b.8.25., and S.26.a.2.5. were continuously occupied by observers.
   3 men were seen all day in a hole at S.20.a.2.5.
   Movement on the roads in the back area was normal.

   (c) Aviation.
   Very little E.A. activity is reported; at 6 p.m. 5 E.A. approached our lines, but did not cross them.

3. HOSTILE DEFENCES.

   New Work.
   A dug-out is being made in the N. bank of the road at X.24.c.0.4.

   Wire.
   Another row of wire has been put up in front of the German trench X.23.d.9.4. to X.23.d.9.5.

4. MISCELLANEOUS.

   A Very Pistol and three cartridges were found on the body of the German Officer who was killed on the morning of the 22nd inst.

5. NEIGHBOURING DIVISION.

   M.G's.
   The Division on our left reports that a M.G. is suspected in a small quarry at S.14.d.5.7., and that a M.G. emplacement is sited at the Southern end of the trench in S.20.a.

   (Sd) W.R. BRANDT,
   Lieut.,
   for G.S., 3rd Cavalry Division.

24th June, 1917.

Examination of wounded Prisoner of 5th. Company 2nd. R.I.R.
who has since died in Hospital.
=*=

Order of Battle.

No knowledge of sector limits or of units on left and right.

1st. Battalion now in line.
2nd.   "   (prisoner's) in reserve in VENDHUILE.
3rd.   "   resting behind HINDENBURG LINE.

Coy. Strength.

About 125.

Method of holding the line.

Front line is held very lightly.
1 coy. per 600 metres.
2 platoons in front line, 2 platoons in support for 48 hrs.
Prisoner cannot describe where the support troops are, but states that they are in a row of dug-outs about 200 - 300 metres to the rear.
When the prisoner's Coy. was last in the front line (about 10 days ago) they held the line S.W. of VENDHUILE.

M.Gs.

Each Battalion has a machine gun "ZUG" attached, of 4 guns each; these are all of the light type.
No regular M.G. emplacements; M.Gs continually moved from place to place. When battalions go back to reserve or rest their M.Gs. do not accompany them. Have never seen M.G. in the front line.

A.Rs.

Prisoner has never seen an automatic rifle on this front, but has heard others speak of them. Cannot say how many the Regiment has.

Wire.

The wire in front of the sap in X.30.a. consists of one belt of 4 strands about 4 metres deep; the wire is not thick and there are many weak places.

Saps.

Prisoner only knows of the one sap in X.30.a., about 4 feet deep, and has not heard that any more are contemplated.

Listening Posts.

Prisoner has heard of listening posts in front of the enemy's wire but has never seen or occupied one.

Last night's raid was to have taken place the night before last, but on that occasion the men refused to go over. Last night 4 sections (32 men) of the 5th. Coy. who were in reserve in VENDHUILE were detailed for the raids under the command of a 2nd. Lieutenant. He could not say whether they all went over from the same line of trench. Prisoner was wounded by the enemy T.M's whose barrage was short.

Prisoner insisted that the 2nd. R.I.R. no longer belongs to the 3rd. Res. Division, but is now an independent unit.

Note. - None of the prisoners had their identity discs or pay-books on them, nor any documents leading to identification.

=*=

Annexe to 3rd. Cavalry Division Intelligence Summary

23rd. June, 1917.

REPORT ON THE ENEMY RAID AGAINST THE BIRDCAGE ON THE MORNING OF THE 22nd. INST.

About 1.10 a.m. on the morning of the 22nd. inst., an officers patrol which had left the BIRDCAGE to reconnoitre a suspected sap about X.30.central returned hurriedly and warned the garrison of an impending attack. At the same moment the enemy commenced a violent bombardment of the BIRDCAGE, BIRD LANE and BIRDCAGE QUARRY, and shortly afterwards a party of the enemy were seen advancing from about X.30.central. None of this party reached our wire, being driven off by rapid fire from rifles and Hotchkiss rifles, and no estimate of the numbers can be given.

In the meanwhile a second party of the enemy approached from OSSUS WOOD in X.29.b. and endeavoured to attack BIRD LANE about X.29.d.6.9. This party was caught by their own T.M. barrage which was "plastering" our wire along that side and none of the enemy succeeded in reaching our trenches. Of this party 3 wounded prisoners were brought in, two of whom have since died (a report of the examination of the 3rd. is annexed) and 7 enemy dead were counted along the front of our wire, including one officer.

The enemy's bombardment was intense for 30 minutes and lasted altogether for about 45 minutes.

From the above evidence it would appear that :-

(i) The enemy intended an attack on the BIRDCAGE from two sides simultaneously.
(ii) The attack from X.30.central failed owing to the timely warning given to the garrison by the patrol.
(iii) The attack from OSSUS WOOD was broken by the enemy's own T.M. barrage.

P.T.O.

REPORT OF WORK FOR WEEK ENDING 29th. JUNE, 1917.

Ref. Map 1/20,000 (57C. S.E.
                  (62C. N.E.

(a) Work completed.

   (i) Damage to BIRDCAGE and gaps mended in wire.
   (ii) Sandbag barricade in QUARRIES in D.1. completed.
   (iii) Outpost in D.1. wire strengthened and repaired.
   (iv) C.T. leading to CATLET post drained and boarded.
   (v) Wire in front of BIRDCAGE improved and fire-bays in C.T. to BIRDCAGE improved.
   (vi) M.G. emplacement at F.5.c.2.8. completed.
   (vii) Bomb Store and T.M.Bomb Store completed in C.T. to G.Post and QUARRY Headquarters.
   (viii) New Headquarters in D.2. Sector at X.21.c.8.3½.
   (ix) C.T.BIRDCAGE — QUARRY and wired.
   (x) 8 T.M.Emplacements in BIRDCAGE.
   (xi) Mined dug-outs at X.22.d.7½.9.

(b) Work commenced.

   (i) C.T.BIRDCAGE — QUARRY.
   (ii) Listening Post at CATLET Post.
   (iii) T head commenced in C.T. QUARRY — BIRDCAGE.
   (iv) Ammunition dump and shelter at X.21.d.9.5.
   (v) 6 shelters in L.Post.

(c) Work in Progress.

   (i) Deepening trenches and C.T. throughout sector.
   (ii) Construction of C.Ts. continued.
   (iii) Clearing berms and improving fire-bays.
   (iv) Draining trenches and laying duckboards.
   (v) Construction of dug-outs at X.21.c.6.1. LIMERICK POST.
   (vi) Dug-outs proceeded with at F.4.a.1.9.

                                   Sd. R.E.Cecil, Major,
29th. June, 1917.   for G.O.C., 3rd. Cavalry Division.

To

    Cavalry Corps.

Report on New Work for week ending
Friday June, 22nd. 1917.

1. OUTPOST LINE.

(a) Work. Saps run out from N. and S. end of front trench in BIRDCAGE (X.29.d.).
Emplacements and recesses for Stokes Mortars and ammunition prepared in BIRDCAGE.
Fire trench (to run from S. end of BIRDCAGE support trench to QUARRY in X.29.d.2.2.) commenced.

(b) Wire.

Tactical rays put up in front of No. 4 Outpost, sited in conjunction with Infnatry M.G. position.
Wire thickened and improved from No. 3 to No. 4 outpost.

(c) Communications.

Communication trench from G.Post to BIRDCAGE now completed as far as QUARRY in X.29.d.2.2., but requires deepening in last 200 yards.
Communication trench from L.Post to new Outpost H.Q. at X.22.d.7.8. completed and drained.

2. INTERMEDIATE LINE.

(A) Work.

Sap for M.G. run out from N. end of K.Post at X.22.c.9.0.
New T fire trench in J.Post constructed (X.28.b.1.2.).

(b) Wire.

Six tactical rays, sited in conjunction with Infantry M.G. position, put up N. of M.Post.
Wire run out from N. of CRUCIFORM POST at X.28.d.5.7. and completed as far as exsisting wire at X.29.b.1.4. (S.W. end of OSSUS WOOD).
Wire from K.Post (X.22.c.9.0) to No. 1 Outpost (X.23.c.7.2) completed and doubled.
This is now double apron.

(c) Communications.

Communication trench from L.Post to new Sub-sector H.Q. (X.21.c.8.4.) completed as far as X.21.d.4.1.

                                            Sd. G.P.Cosens, Major,
22nd. June, 1917.   G.S., 3rd. Cavaley Division.

Copies to :-
    "D" Sector.
    6th. Cav. Bde. Details.
    7th. Cav. Bde.
    8th. Cav. Bde.
    Cav. Corps. (2 copies)

G. 415/2.

REPORT OF NEW WORK WEEK ENDING
FRIDAY June, 15th. 1917.

1. OUTPOST line.

    (a) Work.

        A fire position was made in the East bank of the BIRDCAGE QUARRIES.

    (b) Wire.

        Wire in front of Outpost line - D.2. - made continuous, as far as No. 1 post.
        Wire from 'K' Post to No. 1 Post - 500^x of this has been done - X.22.d.0.0. - X.22.d.8.2.

    (c) Communications.

        C.T. from G.Post to BIRDCAGE QUARRY is completed from G.Post up to X.22.d.85.95.

2. INTERMEDIATE LINE.

    (a) Work.

        No new work of importance.

    (b) Wire.

        The work of putting up tactical rays of wire in X.15.d. was commenced - to join up with the Division on our left.

    (c) Communications.

        New C.T. to M.Post was dug from X.21.a.0.7.
        A new C.T. was dug in the centre of CATELET COPSE.

    (d) Miscellaneous.

        New M.G. emplacements made in front of G. and M.Posts - saps dug leading out to same.
        Dug-outs for Sqdn. HD.'Qrs. made in K. and M.Posts.
        Several Hotchkiss rifle emplacements constructed.

3. Remarks.

        The severe storms necessitated considerable work being done to drain the trenches.

                                        Sd. W.P.Browne, Captain,
15th. June, 1917.   S.S. 3rd. Cvalry Division.

SECRET.   Appendix 9

G. 415/1.

SUMMARY OF WORK DONE DURING WEEK ENDING
FRIDAY JUNE- 8th. 1917.

1.   OUTPOST LINE.

   (a) The BIRDCAGE.

   C.T. QUARRIES - BIRDCAGE deepened and completed.
   Left arm of cross-trench deepened.
   Parapets thickened - trenches drained.
   One good apron of wire completed from G.Post via
X.29.d.2.5. right round the front of the BIRDCAGE and back
to X.29.central.

   It is intended to put up another apron inside the
present one.

   (b) Left Sector.

   Draining, wiring, thickening parapets, fitting in
undercut parapets and widening trenches.
   New C.T. dug from $X.22.c.3\frac{1}{2}.2\frac{1}{2}$. via X.22.c.6.5. and
X.22.d.6.7. to new Outpost H.Q. at $X.22.d.7\frac{1}{2}.9$.

2.   INTERMEDIATE LINE.

   (a) New Work.

      (i) A trversed fire-trench was dug - as a support to
the fire-trenhh, which connects M. and L.Posts - from M.Post
to X.21.b.2.3.
      (ii) A short trench (35^x) was dug behind the Cruciform
to provide sleeping accomodation for the garrison of that Post.
      (iii) General.
         The H.Post support trench was completed.
         Improvement work was done on all Posts.
         Considerable work was done in J.post (CATELET
COPSE). T fire-bays were deepened and fire-steps made. 10^x
of C.T. was dug S. of COPSE. Fire-stepped position for Hotchkiss
rifle constructed in this trench.
      (iv) Communications.
         Communication trenches deepened and duck-boarded.

3.   MISCELLANEOUS.

   (a) Dug-Outs.

   2 very strong baby-elephants were completed in
X.25.a.3.5.
   The new H.Q. for D.1. and D.2. Sub-sectors were
completed.
   2 large elephants are nearly completed for the
Aid Post in EPEHY.
   (b) The R.E. were engaged on improving the water
supply.

                          Sd. W.P.Browne, Captain,
8th. June, 1917.   General Staff, 3rd. Cavalry Division.

To Cav. Corps.
Copy to D.Sector.

Appendix. 25.

Narrative of Events from May 12th. to May 31st.

Reference 1/40,000 and 1/20,000 Maps attached.

Corps Front.

1. The front taken over by Cavalry Corps from III Corps extended from the OMIGNON River to PEIZIERE (EPEHY).
   The defence system consisted of (i. an Outpost line, (ii. an Intermediate line (iii. a second line.

Method of holding Corps Front.

2. It was originally intended to hold this front with two Cavalry Divisions in the line, each having one Cavalry Division in Reserve behind it. The 3rd. Cavalry Division was allotted a position in Reserve to 2nd. Cavalry Division, in the Northern Sector (HARGICOURT - PEIZIERE).
   The 59th. Division was allotted to Cavalry Corps for work on the 2nd. Line.

Readjustment of Front.

3. About May 18th. it was decided to withdraw the 59th. Division and a redistribution of the Cavalry Divisions became necessary.

Distribution of Divisions.

4. In order to arrange for distribution in depth, all four Cavalry Divisions each took over a portion of the line, keeping two Brigades in the front system, with one Brigade in reserve, undergoing training in Western portion of Divisional Area.

Front held by 3rd. Cav. Div.

5. The 3rd. Cavalry Division were allotted the Northernmost Sector of the Corps front, extending from a point 400 yards N. of TOMBOIS FARM to the TARGELLE RAVINE.
   This portion of the line was taken over from a Brigade of the 2nd. Cavalry Division, who held it in accordance with the arrangements outlined in para. 2. The relief was completed by dawn May 25th.
   To the N. from TARGELLE RAVINE the line was held by 40th. and later by 35th. Division of the XVCorps; the XVth. Corps handing over in the early part of June to III Corps.
   To the S. from TOMBOIS FARM the line was held by 2nd. Cavalry Division.

Organisation of Divisional Front.

6. The Sector taken over by 3rd. Cavalry Division was known as D. Sector: this again was divided into 2 Sub-sectors known as D.1 and D.2.
   The whole Sector was in charge of a G.O.C. Brigade, with Brigade Staff, relieved every 9 days.
   The Sub-sectors were each in charge of a Regimental Commander with Regimental H.Q. Staff relieved every 6 days. (see entries in body of Diary and Appendices).

Role of Divisional Staff.

7. In view of the organisation mentioned in para 6, the chief functions of the Divisional Staff were centred in ensuring continuity of policy between successive Commanders of Sector D. and in keeping up liaison with formations on either flank.

8.

2.

Tactical features of front.

8. The principal tactical features of D. Sector were:-

    (i) The high ground running from EPEHY to LEMPIRE in the 2nd. Cavalry Division Area.
    (ii) The spurs running E. and N.E. from this high ground.

The main tactical features held by the enemy on this front were:-

    (i) The high ground about LA TERRIERE which gave direct observation over the area VENDHUILE - LEMPIRE - EPEHY.
    (ii) The KNOLL (F.6.c.) which gave closer observation over the same area.

Troops allotted for defence.

9. For the defence of each Sub-sector, three Cavalry Regiments and one Machine Gun Squadron were allotted.

Owing to the necessity of keeping back a proportion of the personnel for the care of the horses, and also to the basis of the Staff Organisation (viz. One Bde Staff: and 2 Regimental Staffs for each period) it was necessary to draw up special establishments for units to adhere to when actually in the line. These gave a strength of approximately 3 Officers 100 other ranks and 4 Hotchkiss Rifles per Squadron, with 12 M.Gs. per M.G. Sqdn. or a total of 900 N.C.Os and men with 36 Hotchkiss and 12 M.Gs. for each Sub-sector, the frontage of which was approximately 1800 yards.

The establishments laid down are contained in an Appendix to the Diary.

Working Parties.

10. In addition to the troops already enumerated a certain number (about 150) of the Dismounted personnel of each Bdes. were available for work.

These were found by the Brigade in Reserve at the moment, the Dismounted men of the Bdes. joining their units as these Bdes went into the line.

Policy laid down by Fourth Army & CAV. Corps.

11. The general policy in the conduct of the operations decided upon by the Fourth Army imposed a defensive attitude, in view of the wide extent of front to be held.

The Fourth Army Memorandum on the subject is contained in Appendix 15.

To carry out this policy the maintenance of a wide "No Man's Land" was of advantage, in order that the enemy might be prevented from advancing his trench system into close proximity to our own, with the idea eventually of launching an offensive.

To ensure that this wide extent of "No Man's Land" was maintained, a locally offensive attitude by means of patrols etc. was necessary all along the front.

Operations. 12. The nature of the operations undertaken may therefore be considered as having fallen under two distinct headings:-

    (i) Work on the Intermediate Line, which was intended to be the line of resistance; and on Outpost Line.

(ii) Patrolling and constant activity on the part of snipers etc., to prevent any local advance by the enemy.

As regards (i) efforts were concentrated on making the Intermediate Line into a strong trench system, with continuous wire, and also upon making wire continuous along the front of the Outpost line. All other considerations were to some extent subordinated to this at the commencement of our tenure of the line.

The organisation of the work is shown in Appendix 22.

As regards (ii) nothing on a large scale was undertaken, in view of the necessity of first strengthening the line of resistance.

There was however some activity in the vicinity of the BIRDCAGE near OSSUS WOOD, chiefly by means of snipers, which kept the enemy under control whilst this work was being wired.

In all xxxxxxx small offensives of patrols etc., it was impressed upon all ranks that the weapon to b employed was the rifle and not the bomb, which was practically of negligable value in view of the distance apart of the opposing lines.

Artillery.

13. The Horse and Field Artillery allotted for defence of the Sector was grouped under the command of the C.R.H.A. 3rd. Cavalry Division.

It consisted of IVth. Bde. R.H.A.   3 Btys. 13 pr.
B/296 Bty. R.F.A.   18prs.
C/296   "   "   "
D/296   "   "   4.5 Hows.

One Battery 13 pr. was kept in Reserve Training in Western portion of Area.

Owing to the small number of guns on the front schemes of mutual support and for the xxxxxxx concentration of fire on any portion of the front were worked out in consultation with the Divisions on either flank.

In addition to the above the Corps had 2 Groups of Heavy Artillery allotted to it - schemes were worked out for the concentration of fire of Corps H.A. on any given Divisional Sector front. For concentrations on portions of front smaller than this, C.R.A's of Divisions had the power to ask the Heavy Group concerned direct.

3rd. Cavalry Division Intelligence Summary for period -

From 8 a.m. 24th. to 8 a.m. 25th. June, 1917.

1. Operations on Divisional Front.

(a) A raid was carried out this morning at 1.10 a.m. on the enemy trenches from X.24.c.1.7. to X.24.a.2.4. The raid was made by two parties. The right party was operating South of the OSSUS road and the left party North of the road. The right party reached the enemy's wire and laid a Bangalore torpedo which however failed to explode at once and the party was delayed. Eventually the party reached the enemy's trenches and killed some Germans but had to withdraw owing to having exceeded the time limit. The left party cut the first line of enemy's wire and prepared to blow up the main line of wire, but found some white posts marking a track through the wire by which they entered the enemy's trenches.

Three Germans were killed by the advanced scouts and an automatic weapon in a shell hole blown up. The whole party remained in the hostile trenches for some minutes during which time several Germans were accounted for.

The enemy bombarded his own trench in X.24.a.3.8. with trench mortars and it is believed killed several of his own men as hostile fire coming from that direction ceased at the commencement of his bombardment.

One prisoner was taken but died before he could be brought in.

Other identifications were procured showing the Germans to belong to the 2nd. Battalion 124th. Infantry Regiment.

(b) Artillery.

11.50 a.m. our 13 pdrs. shelled OSSUS WOOD.
3.15 - 3.45 p.m. our 13 pdrs. and 4.5 Hows. shelled the enemy's positions in F.6.a. and X.24.c.
5.40 p.m. we shelled CANAL WOOD.
7.20 p.m. we shelled the enemy's positions N. of OSSUS WOOD.

2.   Enemy Attitude and Activity.

(a) Artillery.

12.20 p.m. TOMBOIS FARM was shelled with 77 mm. from the direction of VENDHUILE.
1.35 p.m. 2 rounds H.E. were fired into PETIT PREIL FARM.
2.50 - 3.40 p.m. PIGEON RAVINE and the vicinity of "M" "L" and "K" Posts were shelled with 4.2 cm. and 77 mm.

(b) Movement.

11 a.m. A party of 33 men was seen entering LA PANNERIE NORTH.
2.45 p.m. A party of about 30 men were seen on the GOUY BEAUREVOIR road going Eastwards.
The observation holes at X.23.b.8.25 and S.26.a.2.5. were occupied during the day.

(c) Aviation.

9. - 9.30 a.m. E.A. manoeuvred over our lines in X.17, 23, and 29.
3.50 p.m. 2 E.A. manoeuvred over our lines for about 30 minutes finally coming low down over our trenches in X.17 and firing M.Gs. at the occupants.
8.15 p.m. 1 E.A. attempted an attack on one of our O.Bs. The observer descended from the balloon by parachute, and the E.A. was driven off by our A.A. fire.

3. Hostile Defences.

(a) Work and New Trenches.

Fresh work resembling a new trench can be seen in the sandpit in S.10.c.3.8.

(b) Wire.

A gap in the wire at X.30.a.8.5. has been filled up with a single strand.

(c) M.G..

There is a suspected M.G. Post at X.17.d.6.4.; only used at night.

(d) Miscellaneous.

An air-line has been built running N.W. from LA TERRIERE.

4. Distribution of Enemy's Forces.

Identification.

27th. Division.
124th. I.R.   X.24.a.   equipment.   Normal.

                                                Sd. W.R.BRANDT, Lieut,

25th. June, 1917.   for G.S., 3rd. Cavalry Division.

3rd CAVALRY DIVISION INTELLIGENCE SUMMARY FOR
24 HOURS FROM 8 a.m. 25th to 8 a.m. 26th JUNE.

1. **ENEMY ATTITUDE AND ACTIVITY.**

    (a) **Artillery.**

    1-45 p.m. - 2-0 p.m. MEATH POST and LIMERICK POST were shelled with 4.2.cm from the direction of LA TERRIERE.
    12 noon - 2-15 p.m. LEMPIRE was shelled with about 50 rounds 8" from the direction of LE CATELET.

    (b) **Movement.**

    8-57 a.m. A train was seen at T.19.a.4.8. going in the direction of AUBENCHEUL.
    10 a.m. A heliograph was seen at work for ½ an hour at S.21.b.3.6.
    11 a.m. Signalling with a heliograph and with a white flag observed at S.21.b.3.6.
    6-10 p.m. A fire was seen at S.28.a.1.1. in the vicinity of RICHMOND COPSE, burning fiercely for 15 minutes.
    9-15 p.m. There appeared to be an explosion in the German trenches South of CANAL WOOD.

    The observation hole in X.23.b.8.25. was occupied during the day.
    Road traffic was normal.

    (c) **Aviation.**

    10-30 a.m. One E.A. flew very low over the BIRDCAGE and dropped a white and yellow light. About the same time 2 H.E. shells fell in the vicinity of PETIT PRIEL FARM. The E.A. withdrew in a Southerly direction.

2. **ENEMY DEFENCES.**

    Wire.

    The wire in front of the German line in X.24.a. is broken in 2 places.

3. **MISCELLANEOUS.**

    During the night, the enemy made frequent use of coloured lights, green and red and golden rain.

(Sd) W.R. BRANDT, Lieut.,
26th June, 1917.   for G.S., 3rd Cavalry Division.

3rd. Cavalry Division Intelligence Summary for period

8 a.m. 26th. to 8 a.m. 27th. June, 1917.

1. **Operations on Divisional Front.**

    (a) Patrols.

    A patrol which went out last night from "G" Post confirmed the presence of a small enemy post at the WILLOWS F.5.d.8.4.

    (b) Artillery.

    8.45 - 9 a.m. Our 4.5 Hows. shelled VENDHUILE and MACQUINCOURT FARM.
    9.50 a.m. Our 13 pdrs. shelled CANAL WOOD. 12 rounds.
    10.30 a.m. - 12.30 p.m. Our 13pdrs. shelled OSSUS WOOD and the enemy's trenches in X.30.a. 82 rounds were fired.
    12.30 p.m. Our 18 pdrs. shelled the dug-out suspected to be at S.15.a.15.45.
    1.20 p.m. Our 13 pdrs. shelled the enemy's trenches in X.24.a.
    4.50 p.m. Our 4.5 Hows. shelled VENDHUILE.

2. **Enemy Attitude and Activity.**

    (a) Artillery.

    8.15 a.m. - 9.30 a.m. Our posts North and South of TARGELLE VALLEY were shelled with 4.2 cm. from the direction of KINGSTON QUARRY.
    9.50 - 10.10 a.m. CATELET VALLEY was shelled with 4.2 cm. from the direction of HONNECOURT.
    10.30 a.m. The TARGELLE VALLEY area was again shelled with 4.2 cm. from the direction of KINGSTON QUARRY.
    10.35 a.m. PETIT PRIEL FARM was shelled with 77 mm. from the direction of LA TERRIERE.
    12 noon - 12.20 p.m. PETIT PRIEL FARM was shelled with 77 cm. from the direction of LE CATELET.
    8.30 p.m. - 9.15 p.m. Our posts North and South of TARGELLE VALLEY were shelled from the direction of LA TERRIERE.

    (b) Movement.

    The usual movement of working parties was observed on the HINDENBURG LINE.
    At 8.5 p.m. a column of 8 limber wagons were seen on the VILLERS OUTREAUX - GOUY road at T.20.b. proceeding in the direction of GOUY. Otherwise movement on the roads was below normal.

    (c) Aviation.

    There was very little E.A. activity until the evening.
    7.45 p.m. 7 E.A. flew over our lines in X.28 for about 10 minutes.
    10 p.m. 1 E.A. flew very low over PETIT PRIEL FARM and "G" Post, and dropped light signals.

3. **Enemy Defences.**
    (a) Work and new trenches. More work has been done on the communication trench at F.6.a. and it now joins the front line trench up with the support trench.
    At T.20.central new work can be observed on the BEAUREVOIR - FONSOMME line where apparently a dug-out is being constructed.
    (b) Wire. The wire in front of the sap in X.30.a. has been considerably strengthened.
    (c) Dump. The box dump at S.27.c.9.3. has been slightly increased.

    Sd.M.R. BRANDT, Lieut,
27th. June, 1917.   for G.S. 3rd. Cavalry Division.

3rd CAVALRY DIVISION INTELLIGENCE SUMMARY FOR 24 HOURS FROM 8 a.m. 27th to 8 a.m. 28th JUNE, 1917.

1. OPERATIONS ON DIVISIONAL FRONT.

Artillery.
12-20 p.m. - 12-45 p.m. Our 13 pdrs shelled the enemy trenches in F.6.a.
12-45 p.m. Our 18 pdrs shelled the enemy trenches in X.24.a.
2-0 p.m. Our 13 pdrs shelled S.20.a. (sniping 6 rounds).
3-30 p.m. Our 18 pdrs shelled S.15.b.1.1. (sniping 12 rounds.).
4-35 p.m. A suspected O.P. in S.16.a.6.8. was shelled with 6 rounds from our 18 pdrs.
4-40 p.m. Our 18 pdrs shelled VENDHUILE (20 rounds).
5 p.m. - 6 p.m. The following localities were heavily shelled by our 13 pdrs and 18 pdrs (punishment fire) :-
OSSUS, X.23.d., S.20.d., and S.27.a.

2. ENEMY'S ATTITUDE AND ACTIVITY.

(a) **Artillery.**
8-0 a.m. - 9-15 a.m. Our positions in the neighbourhood of TARGELLE VALLEY were shelled with 77 mm.
12-45 p.m. No. 13 COPSE and the BIRDCAGE were shelled with 77 mm from the direction of LA TERRIERE.
4-40 p.m. CATELET COPSE shelled from the direction of LE CATELET.
5-20 p.m. - 5-45 p.m. F.15. and X.20. were shelled with H.E. and smoke shells which made very little noise on bursting and emitted clouds of white smoke; probably ranging fire.
8-45 p.m. - 9-15 p.m. No.13 COPSE and vicinity shelled with shrapnel.
During the night, about 50 rounds were fired at intervals on the road between "G" Post and TOMBOIS FARM.
During the day, the enemy seemed to be ranging our OUTPOST LINE as if a new Battery had come into position in the neighbourhood of BANTOUVILLE.

(b) **Movement.**
Enemy working parties are reported to be very active in OSSUS WOOD; the sound of timber sawing could be heard and the noise of heavy transport close up behind the line.
In the morning, 3 Officers, with a guide, were seen walking from LA TERRIERE towards VENDHUILE, studying the country with the aid of a map.
Movement on the BEAUREVOIR - GOUY Road in both directions was considerably above normal.
11 a.m. A goods train was seen on the Railway proceeding from GOUY - AUBENCHEUL.
Observers were again seen at S.26.a.2.5.

(c) **Aviation.**
8-45 a.m. 5 E.A. approached our lines, but withdrew without crossing them.
2-25 p.m. 1 E.A. approached our lines.

3. ENEMY DEFENCES.
Work and New Trenches. Work is still proceeding on the suspected new dug-out at T.20. Central.
There appears to be a dug-out in the bushes about S.15.b.1.7.

4. MISCELLANEOUS.
During the shelling of OSSUS by our Artillery, a column of white smoke was sent up about 100 feet. This may have been a bomb or trench mortar dump.

28th June, 1917.

(Sd) W.R. BRANDT. Lieut.,
for G.S., 3rd Cavalry Division.

3rd Cavalry Division Fortnightly Intelligence Summary,
period ending 8.0. a.m. 30th June, 17.

1. **Prisoners captured.**
3 wounded prisoners (5th Coy 2nd R.I.R.) were captured on the night 21st/22nd June.
1 wounded prisoner (5th Coy 124th Regiment) was captured on the night 24th/25th but died before reaching our lines.

2. **Operations.**
(a) <u>General</u>. - The enemy's attitude, with the exception of his attack on the BIRDCAGE, has been purely defensive. No enemy patrols have been encountered, but the enemy has always been found very alert in his front line.
(b) <u>Hostile raid</u>. - At 1.15. a.m. on the night 21st/22nd June, after an intense local bombardment, the enemy attacked the BIRDCAGE from two directions.
One party came from X.30.central and was driven off by our fire - no estimate of their numbers could be formed, as they did not reach our wire. One of our officer's patrols gave timely warning of their approach.
The other party, consisting of 4 "gruppes", endeavoured to come in behind the left support, from the direction of OSSUS WOOD. They were caught in their own T.M. Barrage and did not get through our wire. Of this party, 1 Officer & 7 other ranks were found dead on our wire and 3 wounded prisoners were brought in.
The German Officer and 2 of the men (whose bodies were brought in) were carrying Very Pistols and Flares.

3. **Air activity and places bombed.**
(a) <u>Air activity</u> - remains normal. E.A. usually seen in flights of 5 or 6.
On the 24th June, at 3.50 p.m., 2 E.A. manoeuvred over our lines for half an hour, finally coming down low and firing M.G's at the occupants.
On 3 occasions (24th & 29th June) the enemy has made unsuccessful attacks on our balloons.
(b) <u>Places bombed</u>.- No bombing enterprise was carried out by the enemy.

4. **Enemy work.**
(a) <u>General</u>. - As reported in the last Fortnightly Summary, the enemy appears to have two separate policies North and South of OSSUS WOOD. This would be accounted for by the fact that OSSUS WOOD appears, from identifications obtained, to be the Divisional boundary.
(b) <u>S. of OSSUS WOOD</u>.
Considerable work has been done to the enemy's front line system. The following new work has been undertaken:-
(i)   A new C.T. from TINO TRENCH to TINO SUPPORT has been practically completed - it runs from F.6.a.8.2. to S.25.d.1.4.

(11)

(ii) FALCON SAP has been prolonged and appears to finish in a "T" trench at X.30.a.1.2., a very strong wire fence having been erected in front of it.
(iii) The wire in front of TINO and BELOW trenches has been strengthened.

(b) N. of OSSUS WOOD.
The enemy has done very little work on his front line.
Working parties have, however, frequently been heard about the OSSUS Defence Line and in CANAL WOOD.

(c) OSSUS WOOD.
Working parties have frequently been heard in the E. end of OSSUS WOOD. Sounds of sawing timber are continually heard.

(d) E. of the Canal.
The usual work has been observed on the HINDENBURG LINE.

5. Miscellaneous.
(a) Enemy's Air Line. - A newly built Air-Line can be seen running from VENDHUILE on the crest of Hill 130 in S.28.b. A working party was seen on this line on the 19th June and it is since then that the 13cm. H.V. gun has been active.

This line may possibly be the Battery - O.P. line, and the gun itself is probably in action behind the Hill.

(b) Blind shells.
There are still a large number of "duds" among the enemy's 77mm. ammunition.

30th June, 1917.

Captain.
General Staff, 3rd Cavalry Divn:.

7